On *Client Encounters* and ICON9

'ICON9 has proven an effective way to engage our Applications, Sales and Marketing teams in adopting an efficient, collab ative approach to customer encounter optimisation. The ery practical and the accompanying examples ams to col e ii o dded best practic

Jean-Philippe Lamarcq, VP of les, Professional Imaging e2v technologies, 3 years' field experience

'I thoroughly enjoyed reading *Client Encounters* - it was easy going and informative. Even after many years in the field, I found the book very helpful in laying down the process of our customer relationship. It also highlights points that are difficult to navigate, some of which we may not even realise we are facing!'

**Hayssam Balach, VP of Worldwide Sales
Sonics Inc., 23 years' field experience**

'*Client Encounters* is an impressive training vehicle for handling Customer-Facing interactions—informative, practical content, methodically structured with a best practices approach to addressing real situational challenges, and with great tips on overcoming obstacles and avoiding pitfalls. The examples cited, the overall approachability, topics that resonate and the friendly, useful guidance make the book a delight to read while improving the likelihood of successful client encounters.'

**Camille Kokozaki, Strategic Business Development
20+ years' field experience**

'ICON9 contains the tools and processes you need to prepare, realise and follow any kind of customer interaction. Acquiring this know-how is the best way I know to improve your customer relationships, your support outcomes and, hence, your business.'

**Bernard Godet, Technical Marketing and Support
e2v technologies,**

'*Client Encounters* will assist committed Applications Engineers to become the next self-aware leaders by providing them with the tools to deal with ambiguous environments (in both their organisations and their customers'), to consistently achieve better results, faster. This is the most precious framework that any engineer dealing with customers can find.'
**Alessandro Fasan, Senior Executive Account Manager
Synopsys, 16+ years' field experience**

'*Client Encounters* helps application engineers realise the importance of their role in the value chain, from the factory to the end user. The book is also concise and the tools easy to remember and reuse—they helped me improve my communication both inside and outside of Cadence!'
**Sélim Abou Samra, Staff Application Engineer
Cadence Design Systems, 15 years' field experience**

'ICON9 is the best and the most useful non-technical training I have ever attended. It's a collection of simple and efficient tools to maintain good relationships with customers, whatever happens. These tools are not only useful with customers, they also benefit other professional relationships.'
**Etienne Bouin, Application Engineer
e2v technologies, 15 years' field experience**

'This is a fantastic training system to provide us with great approaches for efficient communication and work. Well structured!'
**Eric Xu, Senior FAE
Xilinx, 14 years' field experience**

'I was lucky enough to take one of Andy's trainings for Application Engineers several years ago—it really impressed me and I still use the simple, pragmatic tools and methods today.'
**Stéphanie Fajtl, Customer Support & Application Engineer
STMicroelectronics, 13 years' field experience**

'The ICON9 training helped me considerably with colleagues, not just with customers. My bug reports and improvement requests now go much more smoothly! I also find it easier to stand up for my interests when with customers, and I have a deeper understanding of the importance and meaning of "win–win".'
Stéphane Gailhard, Customer Support Manager
Kalray, 13 years' field experience

'After following ICON9 training and reading *Client Encounters*, I have been much more structured and efficient when preparing meetings and when talking to prospective customers. It's the simplest tools that make all the difference—they are easy to remember and put into practice.'
David Faure, Managing Director
KDAB France, 12 years' field experience

'*Client Encounters* covers a broad spectrum of concepts and skills very much relevant to technical customer interactions. It presents the tools in a structured, methodical and didactic way, easy to apply in practical real-world situations. Beginners as well as seasoned professionals will find it useful and inspirational.'
Maxime Rocca, Senior Staff Field Application Engineer
Xilinx, 10+ years' field experience

'I had so much fun reading this book and the tools it has given me are great for dealing with my customers. A must read!'
Céline Tranquillin, Business Development Engineer
Aselta, 10 years' field experience

'Having benefited from both the AE training course and the ICON9 book, I believe that the combination makes a perfect package for any CAE or technical manager. The material works for both beginners and experienced people, which means that it's great for improving teamwork.'
Hugo Kuo, Corporate Application Engineering
Dolphin Integration, 10 years' field experience

'I first took Andy's training in 2011, then again in 2014 (by which time it had taken the ICON9 format). It immediately helped me with everything from preparing important meetings to producing complex documents … and I was surprised to find that the second course further reinforced my professional reflexes. I use the tools and the learning on a daily basis, and they save me a lot of time!'
Vincent Prevost, Senior Field Applications Engineer
7 years' field experience

'Clarity, simplicity, effectiveness: the keywords to describe ICON9. The training course really made me question some of my old ideas and the book helped fill the gaps!'
Simon-Alexis Abric, Application Engineer
edXact, 2 years' field experience

'It has been my pleasure to work with Andy on deploying the *Client Encounters* concepts across a large population of Customer-Facing Engineers over the past six years. This book is a great source of fundamental tools that help you deal effectively with any kind of client encounter. Witty and concise, and with a sensible emphasis on the meeting preparation phase, it helps with managing angry customers, dynamic product specifications, last-minute meetings and more. Highly recommended and tested in the high-tech environment. An essential read for all engineers!'
Marion McDevitt, Business Learning Manager
STMicroelectronics

Client Encounters
of the Technical Kind

*How to win, support and challenge customers
… methodically*

Andy Betts PhD, MIEEE

First published 2015 in France by:
Iconda Publishing
57 rue des Maquis du Grésivaudan
38920 Crolles, France
contact@icondapublishing.com

ISBN 978-2-7466-8194-1

ICON9® is a registered trademark of Iconda Solutions EURL in France and ICON9™ a trademark of Iconda Solutions EURL in other countries.

This book is dedicated to Sue, Martin and George.
Thank you for your love and support.

Acknowledgements

I would like to thank the many people who have contributed and continue to contribute to this book project. In particular:

Phil Dworsky, whose generous advice got me off the blocks;
Sélim Abou Samra, for unremitting interest and encouragement;
Adrian Johnson, for telling me straight;
Jean-Philippe Lamarcq, for his shining example;
Marion McDevitt, for support with early training courses and continuing encouragement;
Rod Bark, for great advice and beer;
Michael Horne, for use of his flat, wine and fridge magnet.

I am also grateful to all those who took the time and trouble to read and comment on early versions of the text, especially Alice Reinheimer, Arnaud Parisel, Céline Tranquillin, Corine Vullierme, David Faure, Dieter Rudolf, Emmanuel Pierron, Francis Geay, François Clément, Gilles Depeyrot, Hassan Shafeeu, Hugo Kuo, James Gillespie, Malika Viollet, Richard Betts and Stéphanie Fajtl.

Contents

Preface

'All happy families are alike; each unhappy family is
unhappy in its own way',
Leo Tolstoy, *Anna Karenina*

Not long ago, an encounter with a new client—a VP of Field Operations—reminded me of these words from Tolstoy's *Anna Karenina*. There was nothing extraordinary about him, though he was clearly well adjusted and competent. This impression was reinforced as we got to know each other better—even in the most confusing situations, he seemed to find the path of least resistance to unexpectedly positive outcomes. I have noticed others use similar, uncomplicated methods, with similar, happy results.

On the other hand, I meet plenty of professionals with the opposite tendency. They notice difficulties more readily than opportunities, feel seriously overloaded as a result and, to aggravate matters, get bogged down in non-essential tasks.[1] Their efforts to cope are as varied as their imaginations, in contrast with the simple, uniform approach of the more successful population.

When I shared these observations with others, I discovered not only that this phenomenon had already been noticed, but also that it had a name … the Anna Karenina Principle! In brief, it applies to complex systems where one small thing going wrong can cause big problems: where there is one way to get it right, and millions of ways to mess up.

A technology-driven, commercial environment is a good example of such a complex system. A small oversight or a piece of bad luck can send huge amounts of excellent work down the drain.

So what? Even if this is true, how does it help engineers in this situation?

We can't do much with the Anna Karenina Principle alone, as it is simply an observation. What is missing is a description of the way in which 'all happy Customer-Facing Engineers are alike' and instruction for those who wish to emulate them.

---

[1] Surely all of us are like this from time to time—even my exemplary client.

I wrote this book to fill these gaps. It's based on over fifteen years' experience in the field, exposed to the challenges of Customer-Facing work, developing methodologies for my own use and for the teams that I have managed. In doing this work, I have had the good fortune to collaborate with hundreds of engineers, both in operational situations and in training classes, an experience complemented by research and practice in the field of psychology.

The result is the ICON9® toolkit, a collection of tools and methods to:

- Help engineers *win* new customers and bring existing ones over to their point of view

- Favour *support* outcomes which fully satisfy customers while keeping support costs under control

- Enable engineers to *challenge* their customers in a constructive and low-risk manner

- *Structure* pre- and post-sales work for efficiency, teamwork and continuous performance improvement.

The ICON9 tools and methods have been deployed successfully in multiple companies and types of business, in Europe, the USA and the Asia-Pacific region.

My experience shows that ICON9 is of value to both junior and senior engineers. People with little experience of the field appreciate an end-to-end view of the Customer-Facing aspect of their work, while senior engineers find the structure of the toolkit to be novel and helpful. In particular, the terminology, processes and checklists facilitate mentoring of junior colleagues and teamwork in general.

I hope that you enjoy this read and that you find it valuable.

Andy Betts, May 2015

1. Introduction

Customer-Facing Engineers (CFEs) have a pivotal and immensely interesting role in business. Not only are they, by virtue of their exposure to customers, obliged to stay at a high peak of technical competence, they are also pushed to understand the commercial context in which they work and cope with complex, often intercultural communication problems. While the role has considerable challenges (or, perhaps, *because* it has considerable challenges) the intellectual, professional and personal rewards are hard to match.

But who are these people? 'Customer-Facing Engineer' is not a job title, and the reader might legitimately ask what I mean by 'Customer', 'Customer-Facing' and even 'Engineer'.

What I have in mind, firstly, are engineers working in Field Operations in a Business-to-Business (B2B) context— Applications, Marketing and Sales Engineers are typical job titles. There are many others, since variations of company size, product type, commercial environment, etc. make Field Operations rich with exceptions. Product Engineers, Development Engineers, Chief Scientists and many other technically-savvy folk have to work with external clients too.

I therefore use the term 'Customer-Facing Engineer' to describe any person whose core competence is centred on technology but whose job brings them into contact with external clients.

My ambition in writing this book is to help Customer-Facing Engineers tackle confidently challenges at the interface between technology and communication. I propose a structured approach to the Customer-Facing role, providing not only tools for the work, but also terminology and models that can be customised to suit individual and team needs.

It is a fundamental principle of communication that a message must be adapted to its audience, and this is the main reason for focusing so strongly on Customer-Facing Engineers. Guided by this principle, I have selected (from the vast body of work on human psychology) the concepts that I believe are the most relevant to this audience, organised them in a way that they

1

will find familiar and illustrated them with relevant examples. I present the results in our tribal language, as scientifically as possible.

The second reason for my focus is that customers are a company's most precious asset. The engineers dealing with them must therefore have some formal basis for their actions.

Consider the strict procedures that companies adopt in order to protect themselves from errors in product releases. Hardware and software sign-off checks are onerous, since it is crucial to deliver near perfection to the customer. Similarly, the closer we get to the customer, the greater the need for communication excellence.

Of course, there is no question of adopting communication procedures as strict as the checks for hardware and software. Instead, we require a set of simple tools that give engineers the support they need when they need it and leaves them free to exploit their natural communication abilities. It must protect them from errors of communication on days when they are not on top form. It must give them a set of references for communicating about communication itself, providing them with a greater consciousness of their professional actions and putting them in a

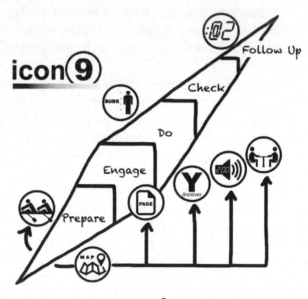

position to improve their own technique over time. Finally, it must facilitate teamwork.

In summary, we need *a set of operational tools and methods that captures successful CFE practices*, and the ICON9® system provides this. It consists of eight tools organised around an Encounter Process, as shown in the diagram opposite. Each tool is represented by an icon, and the process by a compass needle. For convenience, I will usually refer to this ensemble as 'the Toolkit'.

The ninth icon, incorporated into the logo, represents the openness of the system. As will be explained in Chapter 11, users may easily introduce new tools and methods into ICON9, customising it to their tastes and requirements.

The system is based on well-established principles and described using terminology and examples that Customer-Facing Engineers can easily relate to. Let's consider some of the challenges that it addresses.

Challenges for Customer-Facing Engineers

> **In support of sales**
> As a product expert in a design management start-up company, I need to visit a client with my sales colleague to give an introductory presentation. We are expecting to meet about 15 people, including some decision makers. I must therefore sync up with my sales colleague, work on a presentation, prepare answers to the questions that we expect, review areas of the software that I don't know so well, and do some basic research on the customer in question. Of course, I will do these things in parallel with technical work: there is a software release coming up …

In the above example, the challenge is that my mindset for squeezing out the last few bugs from a software release is completely different from the one I need when creating an interesting presentation, and different again from the composed, unhurried attitude that I would like to have when I step up to perform. If I am not careful, I will carry my 'software debug'

3

mindset into the customer meeting and lose my audience in details that are more important to me than to them. The stress caused by the need to switch between these different attitudes and skills (especially if some of the skills are relatively weak) is often attributed to time pressure but, even if this is also present, it is not the main cause. The fundamental difficulty is managing people-oriented tasks in parallel with technical ones.

For a 'happy' outcome, I need tools that help me to rapidly switch between the various tasks. I am used to jumping quickly between half a dozen different tools on my desktop—this is possible because they each have a simple, well-defined use model. If the tasks of meeting preparation, presentation creation and email processing were equally well structured, then I could quickly switch between them too. I could also interleave them with my technical tasks. ICON9 provides the necessary structure.

Addressing customer issues

I have to make a call to a client to discuss a serious bug that he has found in my product. He has invited a couple of colleagues to the call. I feel a surge of adrenaline accompanied by a mixture of unhelpful emotions. On the one hand, I want to defend my product, which I strongly believe in (in fact, I suspect that the client may be the cause of their own problems). On the other hand, I fear the consequences of a conflict. We need to keep this customer happy, but at what cost? As I consider the possibilities, I become even more apprehensive ...

In the second example, above, we are reminded that engineering training has developed my ability to find solutions through the systematic application of theory and process but that, unfortunately, these skills may be obliterated by strong surges of emotion. The danger is that, in my conversation with my customer, I may betray my low opinion of their competence or my irritation with the situation. This could be through a misplaced word, a tone of voice, or my body language. Alternatively, I could overcompensate for the felt emotion, become too passive and end up making unnecessary concessions in order to please the client.

For a 'happier' outcome, I need to have a technique for bringing my emotions under control, and even for using them to

4

my advantage. This is not going to be easy, since emotions are the enemy of technique, and they start with the upper hand. ICON9 not only provides tools that can be applied directly in a case like this (e.g. the SUBROUTINE and TABLE tools—Chapters 6 and 8), it also promotes professional self-awareness. That is, an ability to stand back from a situation and consider it dispassionately. This helps me to learn more from each client encounter and to see the similarities in circumstances that appear, on the surface, to be quite different. Over time, it therefore improves my ability to manage stressful situations.

Taking on a Sales and Marketing role

I have just taken the position of Technical Sales & Marketing Director in a company where, up to now, all Sales and Marketing work has been done by the CEO. With the growth of the company, this arrangement has become untenable and, since I have always taken a lead in communicating about our products, I got the job (up to now, I have had a series of engineering positions).

Already, I can see that my ability to build relationships and my deep knowledge of our products are necessary *but insufficient* for my new role. I have come away from several meetings with a warm fuzzy feeling, but without a useful result.

My third example, above, touches on an area with which many engineers are not comfortable at all—Sales and Marketing. A strong technical background is both a help and a hindrance in commercial work. While subject matter expertise wins credibility, it also represents a comfort zone that I may drift towards at the expense of my communication and business responsibilities. The work environment exaggerates this phenomenon by favouring specialisation, so that we reinforce our primary strengths at the expense of important secondary skills.

This case is a good example of where tools can help me extend my capabilities to address new roles. They allow me to question my intuition, which will tend to lead me back to my comfort zone, and to think and act differently in unfamiliar situations. It's a little like balancing a book on one's head to ensure correct posture. With enough practice, good posture becomes instinctive, and only needs to be checked occasionally. The Toolkit favours better communication posture.

Coping with resistance and politics

I have to go to a distant location for a couple of days to introduce some software to our client's design team. It replaces a system that these designers produced and maintained themselves and I am told that the audience will be hostile. In addition, the group in question is being downsized and reorganised. Though I have no influence on any of these events, they are likely to make my task more difficult ...

In the final example, above, the product that I will be presenting is complex and it is crucial that my audience grasps and accepts some tricky concepts. If not, they will be worse off than before. The cultural and language barriers are significant and it is going to be hard to win them over.

For a 'happy' outcome, I need a robust process for managing the encounter, a good awareness of the visible and hidden aspects of the communication and the ability to make in-course corrections if difficulties arise. It is not always possible to meet one's objectives, and the case described here looks pretty difficult. In these circumstances, it is all the more important that I act knowingly and with method, to give myself the maximum chance of success. As we'll see, ICON9 reinforces my sense of discipline and professional control, allowing me to cope confidently in tough circumstances.

Challenges for Organisations

The examples of the previous section illustrate how ICON9 helps individual CFEs. In practice, the benefits to them are as varied as their backgrounds and personalities. When we then look at the challenges which confront groups and organisations, yet other advantages emerge.

Modern, technology-based organisations need to reconfigure themselves very quickly in response to changes in their environment (i.e. technological and market forces). A common way to do this is to form 'workgroups', 'SWAT teams' or 'task forces'—just three of the terms used to describe a collection of people assembled from across an organisation to tackle an extraordinary issue. In this way, CFEs can be thrown together with other CFEs, with Sales and Marketing colleagues, with Product Engineers, and so on, at a moment's notice. The assignments are generally short term, leaving little time for the 'forming, norming and storming' process that teams are supposed to go through in order to reach peak performance (TuckmanJensen 1977).

Although it can be stimulating to participate in such workgroups, it can also be frustrating. There is little motivation to develop a team culture because of the short-term nature of the arrangement. However, there is an urgent need to work efficiently (fulfilling objectives quickly and economically) and effectively (choosing the right objectives), since the people involved all need to get back to their 'day jobs'.

The value of an authoritative external reference

A newly formed work group of 10 engineers is assigned the task of building a house out of Lego® bricks. The only constraints given are the time available and a fixed supply of bricks, and the group is in competition with others who have been assigned the same task. Further, the members of the group all have some past experience of building Lego houses—some are even quite expert at it— but they have never worked together on such a project before.

I imagine two scenarios. In the first, there is a 10-way debate on how to approach the task while, in the second, a member of the group pulls out an existing recipe for the design and construction of Lego houses. An authoritative external reference such as this would allow the group to quickly get itself organised. Given the time pressure, it is likely that even the Lego-house-building veterans (whose own recipes might have been vastly superior to the one proposed, had they ever been written down) would concede that an imperfect reference is better than none at all. The group could then proceed with the recipe's first step: to choose one of five possible architectural styles, for example. It would then move on to the formula for the number of rooms, according to the number of bricks available, etc.

An external reference can structure the group's work without impinging upon its creativity, allowing it to complete its work on time.

To help groups tackle such problems, the Toolkit provides a ready-made set of references that they would otherwise have to develop themselves: simple, recognisable models, checklists and procedures for key tasks.

Of course, the benefits just described for workgroups also apply to fully fledged teams. When ICON9 becomes part of a team culture, the system acts like a foundation upon which high value-added activities can be built. Rather than spending precious time on the choice of method, the team focuses its energy on areas where it can innovate and differentiate. Having an explicit, clearly articulated way of working also helps with the integration of new members. It is both reassuring and motivating to join a team that is well organised and, for existing members, having a common reference—models, diagrams, vocabulary, etc.—facilitates on-the-job training of recruits.

Cross-team coordination (a real case)

In a company that I worked with recently, the Sales and Applications team was involved in complex negotiations with a customer. There were many parameters involved in the deal, including product specification changes. Fortunately, the team included their engineering group in the planning process, copying information on their intended concessions plan to them. This approach is captured in the TABLE tool for negotiation, discussed in Chapter 8.

In this case, it worked extremely well. The engineering group noticed a number of specification changes, identified as potential concessions, that would have been prohibitively expensive to implement. Since these concessions were spotted before the customer had been made aware of them, they were removed from the plan *at zero cost.*

Finally, the example above illustrates the effectiveness of the tools when used across organisations, beyond individual groups and teams. By triggering the sharing of information, it reduces the chances of misunderstanding and collective error.

Organisation of the Book

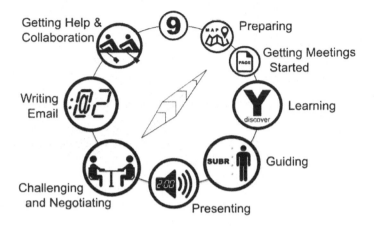

The diagram above shows the order in which tools and topics are addressed and their relative weights (the size of each icon is proportional to the number of pages dedicated to its associated topic). Starting at the top with a brief introduction of ICON9 (already done), the text proceeds in a clockwise direction to return to ICON9 for a final summary. The first three topics—*Preparing* an encounter with MAP, *Getting Meetings Started* with PAGE and *Learning* with DISCOVER-Y—can be quickly learned. The more advanced topics start with *Guiding* and move on through *Presenting*, and so on.

The needle at the centre of the diagram represents the Encounter Process, which is presented in the next chapter and is a reference throughout the book.

Terminology and Scope

Encounters and Meetings

I use the word 'encounter' to describe a period during which I am in contact with a client for a specific purpose, such as selling a product or service, or a discussion of their support needs. An encounter may be face-to-face, screen-to-screen (using teleconferencing), by telephone, or by a combination of these means. It can span several meetings.

A 'meeting' is a single contact event. It can therefore be done using one of the methods just mentioned but, unless my teleconferencing system breaks down and I have to switch, it will not use a combination.

In the text, I use the terms encounter and meeting interchangeably when the discussion applies equally well to either (as it usually does).

Customer-Facing Engineers (CFEs)

The term 'Customer-Facing Engineer' represents any engineer with customer-facing duties, regular or occasional, working in a B2B context. For example:

Field Applications Engineers (FAEs)

Working to balance multiple, often conflicting, requirements in both pre-sales and post-sales roles.

Engineering Consultants

Working with clients from specification through to the delivery of services and custom products. Their work is a mix of direct intervention, training and teaching by example.

Applications and Product Engineers

Working in an office, lab or factory setting, liaising between Design / Research & Development (R&D) teams and field staff, with remote customer contact and perhaps some occasional face-to-face communication.

Design/R&D Engineers

Strongly focused on development tasks, but with a need to transfer their knowledge efficiently to their colleagues and customers.

Sales and Marketing Engineers

Commercially oriented but with strong technical backgrounds, they need to excel in all aspects of communication: to understand clients, to inform them and to negotiate with them.

Engineering Team Leaders/Managers

Guiding development and field operations and wishing to improve processes and outcomes. In FAE Managers and Sales Managers, for example, these roles are often combined with others mentioned above.

Me (the Customer-Facing Engineer) and Aude

I would like to present Myself—easily recognisable from the M of my body shape. I write in the first person a lot, both to express ideas as an author and to put myself in the place of a Customer-Facing Engineer.

May I also introduce Aude, my client, who is referred to as the Audience in many contexts. Aude can generally be thought of as an individual, external client—a customer —though there will be occasions where Aude represents an internal client—a colleague—or multiple clients of either type. I always refer to clients with the neutral 'they', 'them' and 'their', to avoid 'he or she', 'his or her' and other clumsy constructions.

Navigating the Text

Please note the following points:

▸ There are two Tables of Contents (TOCs): a brief one at the start of the book and a detailed one at the end. While the book is not indexed, the Detailed TOC should enable you to find specific points quickly.

▸ Where a chapter includes the description of a new tool, the tool and its use model are summarised in an 'In Brief' section at the end of the chapter.

▸ www.icon9.net contains an online version of the Toolkit, an extended bibliography (with links to references) and other complementary material to the book.

I suggest that, once you have read the book, the Detailed TOC (Annex 3) is a good re-entry point. For sections that are of particular interest, I recommend consulting the associated information and references on the web.

I will be happy to receive comments, questions and suggestions for the book and the web pages.

2. The Encounter Process

'The electron is a theory that we use; it is so useful in understanding the way nature works that we can almost call it real',
Richard Feynman

Like the electron, an encounter is an abstract concept. It cannot be seen directly, and its existence is noticed only because of the effect that it has on the adjacent environment. Electrons produce current and light. Encounters result in progress and emotion (positive or negative, and of varying intensity). Like the electron, an encounter also has a model associated with it, which is the subject of this chapter.

Even if the models that are used to describe human interactions are less precise than those used for physics, they are just as useful when appropriately applied. When people come together in a meeting, they interact in ways that, while not predictable, do fall into a discernible pattern. As I will explain, if certain process steps are not followed, there is a high probability of problems such as resistance, incomprehension and slow progress. Here are a couple of examples:

It isn't just about relationships—process matters too

We finally got an order from Display22 and, in my role as Senior Applications Engineer, I am ramping up the technical support programme for them. Part of this job requires that I get to know their key technical people; I find out who they are and invite them to join my team for a short seminar followed by lunch. This works extremely well—my team is able to make many new contacts with their engineers. We all get on so well, in fact, that a bowling evening is organised (paid for by my company). This is a hit, too. Through close contact we become familiar with the inner workings of Display22 and settle into a comfortable routine, with weekly status meetings followed by a trip to a pub or restaurant.

Eventually, my boss loses patience. 'You've produced lots of random information, and some terrific expense bills', he tells me, 'but I don't see any progress in the account!'

The problem? The client relationship has left us comfortable, but stuck. Although we have done a great job of engaging and finding out what the client's problems are, we have not moved the conversation on to new business and commitments.

My second example is also based on 'Display22', but played out in a different way:

Jumping ahead too quickly

When the order is received from Display22, my first action is to contact the project manager, Ernest Mann, who I know from the pre-sales work. I am keen to have him try out some advanced software options, even if these are not covered by Display22's initial purchase.

I take the opportunity of our first weekly meeting to introduce the subject. He is a little reluctant, citing the load that his engineers already have to learn the basics of the tool. I insist, however, as I know that the advanced options are powerful and impressive. I promise Ernest that I will cover them in the technical training and will install the extra software temporarily, all without charge.

This is to no avail. The Display22 engineers don't look at the extra options and Ernest, rather than being grateful for my proactive behaviour, becomes extremely critical of our software and rather impatient with the support.

The problem? I neglected to engage with Ernest or his team properly and pushed my ideas on them before finding out about their real needs. Furthermore, I focused all my efforts on one person, and ended up alienating him by being impatient!

The Obstacle Course

A client encounter, whether it consists of a single call or is stretched out over several meetings, is an obstacle course.

The first difficulty is the barrier that protects my client from the outside world: they are preoccupied with their

Obstacle 1: 'This is my world'

own plans and activities.[2] I have to overcome any resistance there may be to letting me into their world before I can get the meeting off to a good start.

Obstacle 2: 'You don't know me and my problems'

The next obstacle could be that my client feels they are the only one who can understand their 'unique' problems. I therefore have to find out as much as I can about their situation and convince them that I have fully understood their issues.

Even when my client can see that I have grasped their predicament, they are likely to have their own ideas about the solutions needed. This is the third obstacle: a client who is convinced that they know what they want. I have to overcome this resistance, which often takes the form of 'Yes, but …' responses to suggestions from my side.

Obstacle 3: 'I know what I want'

Obstacle 4: 'Oops, I have to go!'

Once an agreeable solution is found, the final obstacle is the Hurry Monster, which causes everyone to run off from the meeting to do important things, forgetting to capture the results of their passage through the obstacle course together.

---

[2] As mentioned earlier, because the client is referred to as the Audience in several contexts in this book, they are represented by a figure with an A-shaped body in the diagrams.

Steps of the Encounter Process

Since I will be faced with this obstacle course wherever I go, it is critical to have a process for dealing with it.

In the diagram below, I illustrate the work done in the three steps of the Encounter Process where client contact is involved (remember that the person with the M-shaped body is me!).

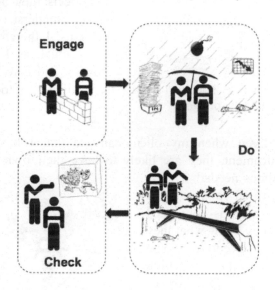

In the **Engage** step, the initial barriers to communication are broken down and an agreement reached on how to run the encounter.

The **Do** step is the core of the meeting, where I explore the client's concerns and try to work out a solution with them.

In the **Check** step, I tackle the Hurry Monster so that we can take the time to consolidate our work and agree to the next steps.

I add **Prepare** and **Follow Up**, where I look after pre- and post-meeting work. The result is a five-step process, as shown in the adjacent diagram.

Follow Up

Check

Do

Engage

Prepare

All five steps are critical, and their order too. Experience shows that, when an encounter goes wrong, problems are a result of process steps that have been skipped or addressed in the wrong sequence.

Prepare

'No plan ever survived contact with the enemy' is a popular military saying, and it may sometimes seem that time spent preparing an encounter is wasted. However, an alternative quote from Dwight Eisenhower illustrates the value of the Prepare step: 'In preparing for battle I have always found that plans are useless, *but planning is indispensable*'.

For example, just a minute's thought before picking up the telephone can make a big difference to the outcome of a call. Encounter preparation time can vary widely, according to the importance of the event, but it's always beneficial.

Joint preparation with colleagues is an important part of the preparation phase. As already mentioned, the 'Me' character can represent a single Customer-Facing Engineer or a number of people in my organisation. In  the latter case, it's vital that this encounter team be aligned on roles, approach, goals and process.

For example, once in front of clients, it will be difficult to exchange information without them knowing. A well-prepared team will have agreed discreet ways of communicating in advance (this topic will be picked up again in Chapter 4).

The tools used in the preparation phase—to agree agendas, anticipate audiences, design presentations, etc.—are even more critical when multiple people are involved in the engagement with the client.

Engage

In this step I come into contact with my client, either physically or remotely. Even if I know them well, the first part of the Engage step is important for establishing good communications, allowing each party to understand the other's level of motivation and their readiness and ability

to contribute. For example, if the person I am meeting seems less energetic and motivated than usual, an effective Engage step will allow me to notice that something is amiss (even if I cannot necessarily understand why).

Note that the obstacle of the initial wall of resistance exists even when people are open to meeting. It is the natural result of the coming together of entities travelling with different speeds and directions. Prior to the encounter, each person is moving independently, and so they have to perform a kind of docking manoeuvre, matching their trajectories.

It is important that I make a positive initial impression through my posture, voice, facial expression, etc. To do this, I need to make sure that I am in good shape—prepared, alert and reasonably relaxed—before the meeting starts. The client's overall impression will depend a great deal on what they pick up subconsciously.

These considerations are just as important when I already know my client. In fact, I should be particularly vigilant if I've already a good working relationship with my client and not take their willingness to receive me for granted. Perhaps they have particular worries today—pressures from work or elsewhere?

Let's start with the 'easy stuff':

- ☐ I should arrive 'on time', interpreting the latter expression according to the local culture (if in doubt, it is best to really be on time!).

- ☐ I take a minute or two to think about the people that I am meeting, to get focused on them.

☐ If I am meeting people for the first time, I prepare for the mental effort of remembering new names and I make sure that I have my business cards ready.

I should ensure that everyone in the meeting is properly *included*. Inclusion is a term that comes from the psychology of the workplace (Schutz 1994) and, in order to ensure a good level of inclusion, it is necessary to take some explicit action. Pre-meeting chat is not sufficient.

How I achieve inclusion will depend on the nature of the meeting, the culture I'm working in, the type of meeting, the duration, the mix of people, the medium (face-to-face or telephone?), etc.

The key thing is that each person should say something, however brief. This ensures that everyone is integrated into the proceedings, that they are acknowledged by the other people present, and they put their other concerns aside to concentrate on the meeting itself.

A simple technique—to break the ice at regular, weekly meetings, for example—is to ask each participant to mention one thing that has happened to them recently. For a three-day technical review meeting with a customer, a more serious introduction would be appropriate.

Whatever method is chosen, taking a few minutes out at the start of the Engage step to achieve this is an excellent practice.

The second half of the Engage step can then transition from the alignment of *people* to the alignment of *expectations and plans*. At the very least, there should be agreement on how much time is available. What's at stake here is both the efficiency and effectiveness of the encounter—the PAGE tool, which is presented in Chapter 4, can be used to facilitate this transition.

Do

I now enter into the core of the meeting. In the context of CFE work, the most common reason for meeting a client is to help them in some way. However, before offering any solutions to my client, I have to find out what their problems are. To do this, I use Discovery—Learning Discovery to find out simple facts and Guiding Discovery to dig deeper and understand the reasons behind my client's stated needs. Spending sufficient time on Discovery is key to effective encounters. Not only does it ensure that my technical understanding of client issues is adequate, but it also allows me to establish the value of any solutions that I may ultimately propose.

Once enough has been learned about my client's situation and problems then, and only then, should I proceed to potential solutions and next steps.

While each encounter unfurls in its own unique way, this simple description leads me to identify three essential components:

▸ **Discover**, in which the information flow is predominantly from the client. I question them about their situation, problems and needs.

▸ **Inform**, in which the information flow is predominantly towards the client. I make suggestions and I may also express my needs.

▸ **Negotiate**, in which the information flow is in both directions. We search for mutually acceptable solutions.

I can picture these three components as a 'DIN triangle', and the core of any encounter will therefore be a dance around the triangle, starting from the D node.

Each of the three DIN components is a major topic in itself, with its own characteristics and tools, and each of them will be discussed in detail later.

Check

Let's say that my encounter has gone well—prepared, engaged and executed correctly, so that everyone is enthusiastic about the agreed next steps.

As always, time is pressing and my client has to run off to another meeting. Also, in spite of our meeting's apparent success, a couple of unfinished items remain and a member of my client's team seems rather withdrawn. Do they not agree with what was decided? Do they need more information or debate? Or is some completely unrelated problem on their minds?

In other words, even the most successful meetings result in a number of open questions and things to tidy up. If they are left in an unresolved state, the good work of the encounter may be undone or even turn out to be counterproductive. For example, a bubble of enthusiasm can quickly turn into a feeling of disappointment if perceived promises are not fulfilled. If a client does not get the solution that they expect for an issue already discussed, then they may not want to talk to me about it again. As far as the withdrawn team member is concerned, have I inadvertently created an enemy? Are they now hostile to my cause and could they undermine my efforts? It is important to sort this out!

In order to make these checks, I need to stall the Hurry Monster. To do this, I have to anticipate his arrival, keeping a tight rein on the meeting agenda from the beginning. This does not mean sticking *rigidly* to the initial plan—who knows where the discussion will take us?—but it does mean:

> ‣ Finding out how much time people have available at the beginning of the meeting (during the Engage step)

> ‣ Bringing the Do step to a halt early enough so that there is time to check for completeness before everyone goes their separate ways.

These precautions in the Engage and Do steps then allow me to tidy up in the Check step. I must check for completeness and agree action points—just like a doctor who makes sure at the end of a consultation that their patient is in a fit state to leave the surgery and that all the necessary medicines have been prescribed.

In summary, the Check step is the essential link between the Do and Follow Up phases, ensuring that:

☐ Agenda points have been covered or we have decided how to deal with them (later, or not at all). In other words, that the *process* is complete.

☐ Goals have been met or we have decided how to deal with them (later, or not at all). In other words, that the *content* is complete.

☐ Next steps, owners and due dates are agreed.

☐ Everyone involved (including myself) is either comfortable with the meeting's outcome or I have noted potential issues, for me to address later.

☐ Anything else that could be considered as a lack of completeness—something not completely dealt with, a concern, a niggle—is noted and, if appropriate, discussed.

Follow Up

The first thing that can happen in this final phase is that all the good work done during the encounter is … forgotten. Everybody's personal Hurry Monster takes over. Other encounters and events occupy available mental bandwidth. Soon, just about the only vestige of our last meeting becomes the date of the next one. As a result, when we all get together again, people's  memories of agreements are fuzzy and a significant portion of the work has to be reviewed—perhaps even renegotiated. Cans of worms reopen, to the frustration of all involved.

What is needed, of course, is a written record of the meeting outcome and its action points. An email of the meeting minutes is usually adequate, and techniques for the effective use of email are discussed in Chapter 9. This record is both a stimulus for agreed actions and, for open items where agreement will be needed on actions, a written record helps to avoid arguments about who said who would do what.

This phase can also serve as a kind of cooling-off period. For example, I might use it to verify that certain ideas which came up during the encounter are implementable. This could involve technical and legal due diligence work—are the ideas OK from the engineering point of view, and do they meet confidentiality, business, procedural and other requirements?

Finally, notice that the Follow Up phase makes the Encounter Process recursive, since other Encounter Processes may result from it. In Chapter 10, I will discuss the business of following up on commitments using assistance from colleagues. This will involve new meetings and, therefore, the Encounter Process.

The Encounter Process		
Prepare	Pre-encounter work	Define objectives, audience and plan (possibly with colleagues).
Engage	First contact with the client (either first ever contact, or simply the initial phase of a new meeting)	Take the time to get in sync with the client, to understand their status and motivation.
	Getting down to work	Align on the purpose, agenda and goals for the encounter.
Do	The core of the encounter	Shift between questioning, informing and negotiating as needed (the Discover, Inform, Negotiate triangle).
Check	The end of the contact part of the encounter	Make sure that all loose ends are tied up and that next steps are agreed.
Follow Up	Post-encounter work	Record the outcome (minutes of the meeting) and perform assigned next steps where possible.
		Deal with known vulnerabilities and pitfalls (e.g. confidentiality, politics, technical failure).

In Brief

✦ Understanding and using the Encounter Process is a prerequisite to consistently achieving effective client meetings.

✦ The Prepare, Engage, Do, Check, Follow Up structure gives us a high-level view of essential meeting steps, and it is critical that none of these steps are skipped.

✦ The Prepare step is always beneficial, even when it turns out to be impossible to implement the plans that result from it.

✦ The Engage step describes initial contact with my client and the business of getting the encounter on track. Both these points must be attended to at every meeting, whether participants know each other and have already prepared the encounter or not.

✦ The Do step is the core of the encounter: Discover, Inform and Negotiate. These three components of the Do step are described in detail in Chapters 5, 6, 7 and 8.

✦ The Check step is used to verify the completeness of the encounter. It is necessary to ensure that all participants are OK with the encounter outcome and that the results of the work are reviewed. All open issues must either be closed, or noted for future closure (next steps).

✦ The Follow Up step completes the work started during the Check phase by recording agreements made in that phase and completing next steps in a timely way, where possible. The work of following up from the encounter inevitably launches new ones, making the Encounter Process recursive.

3. Preparing: MAP

Suppose that, when starting out to an unknown destination, I just type my target coordinates into my GPS and set off. If I am lucky, then I will end up at my destination on time. If not, then, lacking any feeling for the terrain, I could become hopelessly lost (how many GPS users end up in Ashford, Kent instead of Ashford, Surrey, I wonder?—both are just outside of London, but they are eighty miles apart). GPS is a fine system, but the technology can disconnect me from reality.

Be aware that there is an equivalent to GPS for encounter preparation: Get PowerPoint[3] Slides! It has similar mind-numbing properties to its route-finding counterpart and consists of planning a meeting around a slide set, then letting PowerPoint drive the proceedings. Slides are useful, of course, but I should not rely on them to manage meetings. Just as overuse of GPS can cause me to lose touch with the physical terrain, so the Get PowerPoint Slides approach can cause me to lose contact with my clients.

Even though I might still use slides, I use a tool called MAP for tactical encounter preparation.

---

[3] PowerPoint® is a registered trademark of Microsoft Corporation in the United States and other countries.

Giving too much control to the slide set

While working for a company that was prominent in its field, I was involved in a Technical Review Meeting with a major customer. Our preparation was extensive, with a lot of work going into the presentations. Then, when it was all over and the wine and cheese were bringing matters to a close, I asked my champion customer for some feedback.

And why had he been so (uncharacteristically) quiet throughout the proceedings?

'Well,' he replied, 'you spent all day telling us how brilliant you were, and so there didn't seem to be much left to say.'

Oops! We had fallen into the old trap, focusing excessively on the slide set (GPS: Get PowerPoint Slides). As a result, the organisation of the meeting had been far too biased towards our presentations and what we wanted to tell the customer.

In fact, the only encounter preparation that worked out well that day was done by the Sales VP's Personal Assistant. She had baked a fantastic rhubarb pie for the break, and was the only one of us who had the client's real needs in mind!

Strategic versus Tactical Preparation

Broadly speaking, there are two types of encounter preparation: *strategic* and *tactical,* and it is best not to confuse them. If I do, then I may feel well prepared for a meeting when, in fact, I have overlooked one or the other.

Strategic preparation involves assessing my goals and capabilities, as a person and as a representative of my organisation, assessing the characteristics and requirements of my client base, understanding my potential value to this audience and working out how to transform this value into good business. Strategic preparation is usually not associated with a single encounter; it is more likely to be performed for a particular market or account. It is a long-term activity.

On the other hand, tactical preparation (the purpose of MAP) has to be done for each and every encounter. It must combine the results of my strategic preparation with specific information and constraints about the encounter in question, helping me to cope with the unexpected and make predictable progress.

MAP for Tactical Encounter Preparation

The MAP acronym provides a simple way to crystallise pre-encounter thoughts. It stands for:

- ☐ **My objectives** for this encounter, as an individual and for my organisation

- ☐ **Audience** research, background on the people I'll meet, anticipating their questions and concerns, and understanding their company/organisation's strengths and weaknesses

- ☐ **Plan,** adapted to the occasion.

This MAP provides the same benefit as a map for a journey: it gives me a picture of where I am going, makes me less dependent on technological props and helps me to adapt to changing circumstances. Here are some details of each of its three elements.

My objectives

My objectives are:

My objectives

- ☐ Private (not for client viewing)
- ☐ Immediate (concerning just this encounter)
- ☐ Multidirectional (my needs and theirs).

The My in 'My objectives' is there to emphasise that these are *private* objectives which may go beyond the meeting goals that I expose to my client when we meet. They could include, for example, 'Convince my client that their project is doomed' or 'Have my client pay extra for a software upgrade', which are aims that I would not announce openly at the start of a meeting. This is OK—I can remain honest and authentic without being naively transparent.

My objectives are the *immediate* ones for the encounter, rather than for the project with which it is connected. For example, if my project is a $10 million order that we hope to receive next year, my immediate objective will be something like, 'Obtain an introduction to the VP of R&D', or 'Discover any possible obstacles to the sale'. Focusing on immediate objectives *restricts the scope of the MAP to the encounter concerned*.

Finally, My objectives should be *multidirectional*:

- ☐ Information I want *from* my client
- ☐ Information to give *to* them
- ☐ Items to discuss or negotiate *with* them.

Whenever I work with Customer-Facing Engineers on the MAP tool I invariably find that they focus on the information that they wish to give *to* their clients, especially when the encounter preparation includes the production of a presentation. I speculate that this error has several, somewhat contradictory causes, including:

- ▸ An excessive focus on one's own products or technology, and a desire to impress the client with them.

- ▸ Blindness to the many holes in one's understanding of the client's needs and, therefore, to the importance of filling these holes.

- ▸ A misplaced or exaggerated desire to please the client.

All three can be resisted by ensuring that My objectives are multidirectional.

Of course, if I am working in the encounter with colleagues, then 'My objectives' means our joint objectives. In fact, MAP is particularly effective for collaborative work: it requires almost no time to learn and it provides a simple structure and order for group discussions.

Audience

The term 'Audience' is used here to mean the set of clients expected at the encounter. The Audience could also be a 'real' audience, in the sense of an audience at a seminar or training course.

Key data on my audience includes:

- ☐ Names, affiliations and connections to other people, organisations and projects
- ☐ Questions to anticipate and obstacles that may arise
- ☐ Aims and priorities of their organisation (see Chapter 8 and the importance of understanding intentions)
- ☐ Unknowns about the audience.

It is crucial to 'put myself in the audience's shoes'. I can do this by visualising my audience, or remembering a conversation that I have had with them, or perhaps by talking about them to someone. Just so long as I focus outwards, towards my audience, rather than retreating inwards, absorbed by my own preoccupations.

To anticipate the audience's state of mind, consider their:

- ☐ Situation: including their perception of that situation
- ☐ Problems: their issues and concerns
- ☐ Needs: what they want and what they expect from me.

These three simple points are crucial to client conversations, and they are discussed in detail in Chapter 6.

If the encounter is particularly important and an in-depth analysis is desired, then there are many tools available for this (for example, a web search for Stakeholder Analysis will reveal many ways to analyse an audience).

Just as important as the accuracy of my analysis is the effort taken to get the audience in mind. Experience shows that this pays off handsomely when the client meeting takes place. I get in tune with my audience much more quickly since my neural equipment is already up and running the right program.

What if I don't have the time to do any real audience preparation? Even if my call is in just two minutes, then I still have time to form a mental picture of the audience—their Situation, Problems and Needs—and push other preoccupations to the back of my mind.

Plan

The Plan must take a form that is suited to the task, and I can choose any planning tools that I like, or none at all. As already noted, even if the planning process is always valuable it is often impossible to put plans into practice. They may become out of date even before the planning spreadsheet is closed and emailed out.

Cooper and Castellino articulated a *minimum* requirement for an effective plan (CooperCastellino 2012). I call this a *First Move* plan and it consists of just:

☐   A list of tasks to tackle (not prioritised)

☐   A decision on which of them to do first.

The First Move approach is not a panacea, but it can be a great panic-killer, allowing progress in complex situations that are nearly overwhelming.

As Cooper and Castellino wrote:

People are often surprised to find that having tackled the first thing, many of the other actions identified don't even need to be done. Yes, things change and people find themselves achieving their outcome in ways they hadn't known were possible. For example, think about a time you prepared for a difficult conversation. You may have had a clear outcome, worked out all the things you wanted to say and what to say first. After you said that first thing, a conversation ensued that you certainly didn't predict. You responded to what the other person said, and the conversation took a very different direction—yet you still met your outcome.

A First Move plan is not an easy way out either. It still requires careful thought and also the commitment to get on and tackle whichever task is identified as being the most important!

If something more elaborate than a First Move plan is called for, several of the tools in this book are designed for use with MAP, and they plug into its Plan step. This use model is described in the 'MAP as a Front End to Other Tools' section, on page 34.

Complex Situation, Simple Tactics

Strategic versus tactical, MAP-based preparation

I have just joined a company that makes robot arms. My strategic preparation for the job starts with my capabilities, which, I learn, are to produce light, robust, intelligent robot components to specification. My organisation has experience with industrial assembly, food sorting and military applications, though the range of possible uses for the robot arms is vast. At the personal level, I have a mix of electrical and mechanical engineering expertise, some of which was acquired through formal training, and some through an obsession with micro mouse competitions—racing custom-built electromechanical mice through a maze.

Our customer base—the audience—consists of Original Equipment Manufacturers (OEMs), who assemble end products from components provided by their suppliers. They are technically expert and prefer to keep us at a distance from the end customer (their clients) by reducing their requirements down to purely technical specifications. With the exception of the military projects, project lifetimes are around three to four years, and design cycles for new products are 12 to 18 months.

My company has developed a number of ways of interfacing with the OEMs. It first proposes a demonstration of our technology, using a purpose-built demonstration robot. If things go well, and since the technology is complicated, we then offer a two-day workshop, from which a specification should emerge for use in commercial negotiations. Once the OEM has become a customer, we then propose a support process that uses online tools.

The above three paragraphs give an idea of the type of information that figures in my strategic preparation of my work to support the robot arm business. Now suppose that an unexpected event appears on the horizon: a meeting request from the European Space Agency (ESA), who are interested in fitting a robot arm to a moon lander (not our Moon, a moon). I will need to present technical information about the robot arms, and maybe also tell them about our technology roadmap.

Continued on next page ...

cntd.

If I were to base my preparation on existing slide sets, then I would be starting from a presentation that explained our capabilities to an OEM audience and which led up to the proposal of a demonstration, followed by a two-day workshop. The technology roadmap would also be biased towards the characteristics of the OEM market—three- to four-year product lifetimes and 12- to 18-month design cycles. Instead, I define the following MAP:

My objectives: (1) Understand the ESA project model, particularly the differences with the OEM one, (2) show technical credibility.

Audience: (1) I need to check the ESA project timescales, which I believe are five years plus, (2) I need to check how they address risks —I expect them to be conservative and risk-averse, given that reliability in their systems must be a strong requirement.

Plan: (1) Agree agenda and goals in advance, by mail, (2) find out if we have any links, however tenuous, with aerospace projects, (3) have ready a short presentation focused on technical capabilities, rather than applications examples (all our material for the latter is irrelevant).

In the above case, the extended description of the overall situation and strategic considerations contrasts with the narrow focus of the MAP-based preparation.

A simple variant of the above case is easy to imagine: suppose the ESA meeting request is received with extremely little notice. Further, it arrives on a day that's already crowded with important tasks. Even if the only pre-meeting planning that I have time for has to be jotted down on the nearest scrap of paper, MAP still helps. This 'back of an envelope' MAP is slightly modified from the previous one, due to the rushed circumstances.

M: Understand the ESA model (esp. diffs with OEM one)
Tech credibility
Have bench data ready ↗ + spec q'aire

A: Risk-averse?

P: Set expectation that this is a pre-meeting

33

For the Plan part, I decide to play for time by suggesting that the meeting be treated as a preliminary to a later and, by implication, better prepared affair. Given the short notice, the only data I can think of that it is suitable (and safe) for this meeting is from some benchmarks that show our technology in a good light. I also have a list of questions on the client's technical requirements (the 'spec') that we could use to structure the 'discovery' part of the meeting (see Chapters 5 and 6 for more on Discovery techniques).

The tactical preparation of MAP helps me to focus on the key points that are needed here and now. Instead of my long-term strategy, I define my *immediate* objectives for the encounter. Aware of gaps in my knowledge about the client, I aim for a *multidirectional* exchange of information. Rather than a general idea of the market or an account, which was the focus of my strategic preparation, I now *focus on a specific client.* Instead of thinking of all the things that I might propose to my client, I *plan a particular action*—a presentation of a certain product or the negotiation of dates and resources, for example.

In summary, when I need to prepare a specific encounter, MAP helps me to crystallise the most important information and actions from the mass of data available. It provides a concise structure for my thoughts, making them clearer to me and easier to share with colleagues.

MAP as a Front End to Other Tools

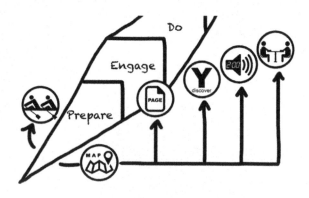

For the following tools:

- ▶ PAGE
- ▶ DISCOVER-Y
- ▶ TWO-MINUTE MESSAGE
- ▶ TABLE
- ▶ OAR

… their use model starts with a definition of My objectives and Audience; then the Plan part of MAP is implemented by the tool in question. For example, the TWO-MINUTE MESSAGE is a tool for planning the content of presentations, and it produces a short synopsis (a message that can be read out in two minutes). Before I start writing this synopsis, however, I have to define My objectives and Audience for the presentation.

This relationship between MAP and the five tools mentioned is represented in the diagram of the ICON9® system opposite. This organisation simplifies the Toolkit, since the 'M' and 'A' parts of MAP do not have to be reinvented for each of the tools to which it 'connects'. They just reuse the terminology and methods discussed in this chapter to define the objectives and audience associated with their use.

Keeping It Simple

> *'It seems that perfection is attained not when there is nothing more to add, but when there is nothing else to take away'*,[4]
> Antoine de Saint-Exupéry (aviator and writer)

MAP is so simple that I used to feel uneasy about calling it a tool. Surely people would expect something more elaborate than these three letters? Engineers are used to rocket science, and the customer-related difficulties they face are extremely complex. Suggesting that MAP will help them seems like offering a hammer to someone trying to defuse a nuclear bomb!

However, my experience has shown that the brevity of MAP is a real, practical asset. It would be quite easy to augment the

---

[4] Original text (Saint-Exupéry 1939): Il semble que la perfection soit atteinte non quand il n'y a plus rien à ajouter, mais quand il n'y a plus rien à retrancher.

acronym with complex, subsidiary tools that formalise the different aspects of one's objectives, audience and plan. However, such complications would kill the spirit of the tool, which is that the key to preparation is *not* to think of everything. *It is to avoid overlooking anything really important.*

The advantage of simplicity is particularly evident when several people collaborate to prepare a meeting or a call. MAP allows us to exchange ideas quickly and not to overlook some crucial basics.

The latter point is just as important when some of the people concerned with a meeting don't actually attend it. MAP is then invaluable for the meeting debrief (in the Follow Up phase). If the MAP checklist that was agreed before the meeting is used to structure the minutes, then the absentees can quickly see which objectives were attained and which were not, how the audience turned out to be compared to expectations, and whether or not the original plan worked out.

I use MAP all the time and can vouch for its effectiveness. Even so, I am amazed by the positive feedback on the tool that I have received from training courses and workshops. In spite of (or perhaps because of) its simplicity, it is probably the most widely adopted of all the tools that I share with CFEs.

So, put aside that GPS and start preparing your next client encounter with a MAP!

In Brief

✦ Tactical preparation crystallises the output of long-term, strategic preparation into a concise form for a specific encounter: My objectives, Audience and Plan.

✦ My objectives are:

- Private (not for client viewing)
- Immediate (concern just this encounter)
- Multidirectional.

✦ Multidirectional means:

- Stuff that I wish to discover *from* my client
- Information to give *to* them
- Things to negotiate *with* them.

✦ To get the right focus on my Audience before an encounter, I assess their Situation, Problems and Needs—my perspective and theirs. Other tools, such as DISCOVER-Y (Chapter 5), may help me to anticipate the Audience's viewpoint.

✦ The Plan can be a simple 'First Move' plan, or it can be implemented using other tools.

✦ MAP may be used in combination with the tools PAGE, DISCOVER-Y, TWO-MINUTE MESSAGE, TABLE and OAR.

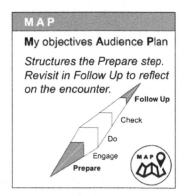

MAP

My objectives Audience Plan

Structures the Prepare step. Revisit in Follow Up to reflect on the encounter.

Follow Up
Check
Do
Engage
Prepare
MAP

4. Getting Meetings Started: PAGE

'You don't manage time, you manage yourself within time',[5]
François Delivré

Persuading a client to take the time to meet can be a difficult task in itself. Having succeeded in organising a meeting, it is therefore extremely important to make best use of the time reserved for it. Furthermore, since my clients will also consider this time to be precious, effective management of the proceedings is a good way to build credibility with them.

 A necessary condition for effective meetings is to get off to a good start. This means reaching agreement on the main meeting parameters so that there is a reference to steer it back to if the discussion ever strays off course. This is where the PAGE tool comes in. It aligns the expectations of those present, and gets them onto the same page.

The PAGE Acronym

PAGE stands for:

CHECKLIST

☐ **Purpose:** Why are we meeting? Is it to share information, plan something, review something, etc.?

☐ **Agenda:** How are we going to work? How will we organise our time?

☐ **Goals:** What are we aiming to achieve *with this meeting*? (a list of specific points)

☐ **Endorsement:** Does everyone agree? Are there other points to add?

---

[5] Original text (Delivré 1997): On ne gère pas son temps, on se gère soi-même dans le temps.

The first three points may be prepared in advance of the meeting, perhaps in collaboration with the client, but they must always be revisited in the meeting itself.

The difference between 'objectives', 'purpose' and 'goals' is important in this context. My objectives, as explained in the previous chapter, are private (hence *My* objectives). They are to be prepared in advance of the meeting, in collaboration with the appropriate colleagues. They may well include statements about my clients, and they are not intended for them to see. For instance a valid objective is 'We will try to get the client to accept a reduced level of on-site support', but it's not something that I would announce at the start of the meeting.

Purpose and Goals, on the other hand, are public. Defining the Purpose of a meeting replies to the question 'W*hy* are we having this meeting', whereas setting the Goals answers 'W*hat* will we achieve by the end of this meeting?' The Purpose of a meeting might be 'to discuss the proposal for on-site support changes', whereas the Goals of the same meeting might be: '(1) agree where on-site support is essential, (2) agree where remote support is acceptable, (3) identify people outside the meeting affected by this issue, (4) set a date for a teleconference to discuss an updated proposal.'

For the Agenda, there are two basic things to decide: the order of topics and the time to allocate for each. When setting an Agenda where both parties are expected to present material, I

The danger of going first (a real case)

A Customer-Facing Engineer had presented some character recognition technology to a client at the beginning of a meeting. During the presentation he explained that the colour contrast between text and background had to be reasonable in order for the system to work. 'But that should not be a problem', he said, 'because, for instance, no idiot would write white characters on an orange background.' Unfortunately, his presentation was before his client's and when the latter stood up to present, everyone saw that their text was white, and their background orange. Oops!

Moral: do everything possible to start with Discovery and, in particular, try to have the agenda organised so that clients present first.

endeavour to have my client present before I do, to allow me to take their view of the world into account when I speak. If the client insists that I go first, as they often do, then I present only limited information at first. After they have presented, I might follow on with relevant, more detailed material.

Several other guidelines for the Agenda aspect of PAGE depend on the Encounter type (above all, its length) and they are discussed in the next section.

The final point in the checklist—Endorsement—is a reminder to get explicit agreement on the Purpose, Agenda and Goals before proceeding with the main business of a meeting. It gives everyone in the meeting an opportunity to ask for modifications to the Purpose, Agenda and Goals, and allows the person driving the meeting to check that they have the attention of all participants.

Please note that, when asking for a confirmation of the Purpose, Agenda and Goals, the question 'Is everyone OK with that?' is not the best one to ask. It is a closed question which risks getting polite, rather meaningless agreement, since people may feel that to say 'no' would be rude (at least, in some cultures). I should therefore try to give my clients and colleagues a real opportunity to have their say by asking an open question, such as 'Do you want to change or add anything?'

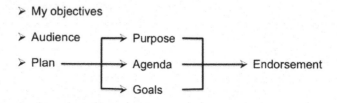

The ideal use model for PAGE is illustrated above. If time allows (see the next section) the Purpose, Agenda and Goals of an encounter are thought out in advance, as a part of the Plan step of MAP. They are then endorsed by all concerned at the meeting itself. How this turns out in practice will depend on the circumstances of the encounter, as will now be discussed.

PAGE for Different Types of Encounter

Short Meetings and Calls

For minor encounters—meetings and telephone calls arranged at short notice, for example—I use MAP and PAGE to get my thoughts straight just before the event. It is quite likely, however, that a significant part of the meeting's organisation, especially the Agenda and Goals, will not be addressed until participants get together. I therefore use what information I have (typically an email thread) to do some modest preparation. This at least helps me to make the mental switch to the people and business of the encounter. I therefore arrive well prepared, given the circumstances, and in a position to take the lead if necessary.

As noted in Chapter 2, there are essentially two parts to the Engage step: an initial 'greeting' part, where participants get in sync, and a 'transition' part that gets the main work of the encounter started. PAGE is invaluable for this second part, especially for meetings and calls that would otherwise have little structure. The tool is essentially used 'on the fly', to help make sure that the minimum organisation is in place before the main discussions begin.

For example, the *absolute minimum to know about the Agenda* is the total amount of time available. It takes only a few seconds to check this. Similarly, it should not take long to agree on the Purpose and Goals, and if it does, then surely it is important to take that time!

Encounters Involving Significant Preparation

For encounters where a detailed agenda is negotiated or, at least, exchanged in advance, the work related to PAGE is shared with my external and internal clients ahead of the meeting. Email is often used to agree on an Agenda, and the Purpose and Goals can be inferred from the related correspondence. I should check that all three items are agreed.

As for short meetings, *the key to getting the meeting on track is to have PAGE used for the transition from the Engage to the Do steps.*

I stress this point because a common mistake at the start of well-prepared encounters is to announce the pre-agreed Agenda (often by displaying it on a slide) then move directly into the main part of the meeting (which usually means the continuation of a presentation). This only works if everyone in the room (physical or virtual) was involved in the agenda preparation, and if nothing has come up since. I would not normally bet on this, which is why the 'E' of PAGE is so important.

Even in situations where the Purpose, Agenda and Goals probably have everyone's approval, a presenter can reinforce contact with the audience by pausing to check. Both the presenter and the audience will be more comfortable if this is done.

Sounding natural

When using PAGE, there is no obligation to say the words 'Purpose', 'Agenda' and 'Goal', of course. For example: *'Good morning! As I think you know, we are here to discuss the content of the next product release (P). I would therefore like to start by gathering everyone's ideas and then setting some priorities (A). Since we have only an hour available (A), I suggest that we try to agree on the top 10 items today (G1) and arrange for a further meeting where we can review the list and plan the work in detail (G2). Are there any other suggestions or comments before we get started, please? (E)'*

Active versus Reactive

So far I have described the use of PAGE for actively driving encounters. A second way to use the tool is in a reactive mode, turning it into a defensive weapon. By this I mean for situations where someone else has taken the lead of the encounter.

In such circumstances, my familiarity with the Encounter Process and the PAGE tool helps me to quickly see whether there is an adequate transition from the Engage to the Do steps. If not, I can try to get things back on track with a specific request. For example, 'Would you mind if we worked out an agenda before getting any further into this discussion ...?' or, 'Could we check how much time everyone has available before we go any further?'

The Role of Roles

Roles for Working Together as a Team

Use of roles is important when working together with colleagues in a meeting. Suppose that I go to see a client with my manager and a Salesperson. To be well coordinated in the meeting, we should discuss beforehand both the roles that we will adopt and how we will communicate during the meeting without necessarily drawing the attention of the client.

Typically, one person is assigned the role of leader. Another might take responsibility for recording what happens, and a third the job of watching for activity outside of the main part of the discussion. Frequently it's better for the manager not to get involved in the discussion, as that leaves an elegant way to have a second opinion if the discussions are deadlocked.

The most important private communication or signal is 'Stop!'. For example, we might agree that raising one's pen is a sign that a colleague should stop talking—perhaps to let the client respond. Another useful signal is 'Slow down!'.

These are simple points, but they have to be thought of before a meeting starts, for obvious reasons.

Roles for Keeping a Meeting on Track

Let's assume that the Purpose, Agenda and Goals of a meeting have been agreed by the participants. Then what?

It sometimes helps, particularly for major encounters, to think carefully about what to do if the discussion strays away from its reference course, and to have a plan for bringing it back. Usually, this is the task of the meeting chairperson—the individual who either explicitly or implicitly has been assigned to lead the meeting. This person's main job is to animate the meeting so that the knowledge and experience of its participants are used to best effect. They are therefore fully occupied with the content of the discussion and the needs of the people involved. Is this person really able to keep an eye on the clock, the agenda, the goals and the meeting minutes all at the same time?

To increase the chances that the Purpose, Agenda and Goals agreed at the start of an encounter are respected, it is sometimes a good idea to lighten the load on the chairperson by assigning roles to other participants.

Standard roles are chairperson, timekeeper, process manager and scribe (minute taker). In large meetings, the chairperson can only possibly perform one or two of these roles adequately.

The role of process manager may need explaining. It involves managing the subprocesses in the meeting, such as discussions, brainstorms and presentations. For example, a process manager might suggest that, to collect ideas for XYZ, everyone should speak in turn until each person has had their say. This will ensure that everyone is able to contribute. An alternative process is to pass an object around—a ball, a plastic giraffe … anything!—and that only the person with the object is allowed to speak. It is the role of the process manager to ensure that such mini-procedures are agreed and respected.

In my experience, the explicit assignment of such roles is not common practice in industry. Sometimes, a well-run meeting starts with an agreement on who will take the minutes, and everyone is relieved when this happens (except maybe the 'volunteer'). I suggest that, to keep encounters aligned with their Purpose, Agenda and Goals, it is worth being aware of other roles and, where appropriate, making them explicit in the organisation of an encounter.

Gaining time by managing the source of the problem

At the beginning of a training course, someone asked if time management would be covered. I had to explain that it would not: there was no such module in the course.

The person who had raised the question came up to me at the end of the course and said, 'You were wrong: your system is going to save me a lot of time, since inefficient meetings are a big source of my problems. Running them more effectively is key to improving my time management.' This makes sense, of course. Gaining better control over meetings is a good way to save time and defeat the Hurry Monster!

In Brief

✦ PAGE is used at the end of the Engage step of the Encounter Process to transition from greetings to getting down to work.

✦ The tool can be used in short, impromptu meetings, or for much longer ones.

✦ It can be used on the fly (where no preparation was possible), or prepared in advance of a meeting.

✦ It can be used in proactive mode (to drive a meeting) or reactive mode (when participating but not leading).

✦ MAP and PAGE are used together, PAGE being a method for implementing the Plan part of MAP when preparing an encounter.

✦ My objectives, Purpose and Goals are distinct. My objectives are private, Purpose answers the 'why' question and Goals the 'what' question.

✦ The absolute minimum definition of an Agenda is the time available for the meeting.

✦ Having roles assigned to meeting participants can help the chairperson to keep the meeting to the plan captured by PAGE.

✦ 'Start with everyone on the same PAGE' is an easy way to remember this tool.

5. Learning: DISCOVER-Y

'There don't hardly nobody listen, and it's so easy! [...] and there's one more part to this one [...] they ain't nobody was ever insulted by a question',
Fauna, the whorehouse owner, priming one of her girls in Steinbeck's *Sweet Thursday*

Discovery is a technique for finding out what I need to know from my clients in a way that moves the conversation forward, to the benefit of both parties. As the quotation shows, this is not rocket science and it applies to all sorts of commerce. Nevertheless, in my enthusiasm for what I am explaining, it's easy to forget the importance of questions. Fortunately, an understanding of the Discovery approach, underpinned with some simple tools and methods, helps me to achieve a good balance between listening and speaking.

Discovery has many characteristics that one might *not* associate with engineering: it is an art rather than a science; it is more associated with commercial work than technical; its objectives are often indirect (relationships and influence) rather than direct (facts and figures). However, I suggest that Discovery can be of immense help to Customer-Facing Engineers, since (1) getting good data is a prerequisite to solving any technical problem, and (2) it is often much easier to persuade a client to accept a technical solution with an indirect, Discovery-based approach than with a head-on, logical explanation.

Advantages of Discovery

To perform Discovery I must take a questioning stance, especially at the beginning of the Do phase of the Encounter Process. This means that I will tend towards asking clients questions rather than explaining things to them. A major advantage of doing this is that it's *guaranteed to hold the client's attention*.

People are much more attentive when being asked questions than when being told facts. In school, it was easy to stop listening and gaze out of the window when the maths teacher droned on at the front of the class. However, when they directed a killer question at me, I suddenly paid attention!

Similarly, taking a Discovery approach helps grab and retain clients' attention. From this point, it is a small step to influencing their view of a situation and moving their opinion in the 'right' direction (please also see the discussion on the difference between influence and manipulation, in Chapter 8).

Further, if I listen carefully to my clients with genuine interest, then *they will be more open to my arguments and more likely to accept my recommendations.* This is a question of confidence—their faith in my ability to help them will strongly depend on how well they think I have understood their situation. It's also a question of the investment that they make in our relationship. Once they have committed time to our conversation, then they will wish (probably subconsciously) to justify their

---

My client invites me to present

I am in a pre-sales situation and the prospect has invited me to present our design services.

I do what I am asked, and present my slides. The prospect is happy, asks lots of questions and then rushes to their next meeting (dutifully obeying the Hurry Monster). They seem satisfied, and I feel that I have made a good presentation. My colleagues congratulate me.

This kind of meeting is almost always a good investment for the prospect, but not necessarily for me. Potential clients are happy to obtain information at zero cost. They don't have to reveal very much and, thanks to the information that I provide, they improve their negotiating position with respect to both me and my competitors. On the other hand, I may miss an opportunity to learn about their business and project needs, how my services line up with those needs and how they compare with my competition. Furthermore, although I will certainly explain the main features of my offer, I am unlikely to pinpoint (or understand) its main benefits for the prospect in question.

Since, in this case, I was explicitly asked to present our services, I should have pushed back a little and done some Discovery. For example, I could have explained how important it was for me to understand more about the prospect's situation before I started my presentation.

---

decision to do so. Every time they decide to answer one of my questions, then their level of engagement grows.[6]

A common reason for failing to do enough Learning Discovery (i.e. talking too much!) is a desire for control over a conversation. As I write, I am reminded of an exhibition that I went to just a couple of days ago. As I went around the stands, learning about the Internet of Things, I talked with the Customer-Facing Engineers running them. To find out what I needed to know, I simply asked a banal question, and this triggered most of

---

A client complaint

Consider the case where my client has a complaint. Let's say that my company managed to sell them some software but that it is giving problems, and they are furious. Really angry.

They summon me to their offices to give me a piece of their mind and, into the bargain, insist that one of our engineers stay on their site for as long as the bugs are not fixed.

Discovery may seem irrelevant here, since there is no need to encourage the client to talk. Quite the opposite: my problem is to get a word in edgeways!

However, good Discovery is absolutely essential in these circumstances, if hard to do. My concern will be to calm the customer, regain their confidence and retain their loyalty. It will also be to minimise the impact of the crisis on me and my company. In particular, I don't want to agree to putting an engineer at the customer's site for 100% of the time—my resources are far too precious for that.

The first thing to do is to listen, and to do this until the client returns to a normal, calm state. Only once this has been achieved can the conversation move forward constructively.

I then need to understand what has gone wrong with the product (the technical view) and what impact this is having on the client from the human and business points of view. Of course, Discovery is the key to finding these things out. By adopting a questioning stance and, above all in these circumstances, avoiding premature explanations and solutions, I facilitate a calm, constructive and productive conversation.

---

[6] (JouleBeauvois 2002), after research by Kurt Lewin on our tendency to stick with our decisions, especially those we consider to have been made of our own free will.

An internal meeting

Consider the example of an internal meeting where I wish to persuade a manager in my own company to send a Product Engineer to help in my account for a few days. The reason is that my customer is putting me under a lot of pressure and I cannot satisfy their crazy requirements on my own.

The meeting opens with my colleague greeting me: 'Hi there! I see that you are having some problems with XYZ. What's up? What do you need from me?'

It would be natural to answer the question directly, explaining my woes in detail and asking for what I need. *That could work, but very often the result will be sympathy from my colleague, accompanied by a stout defence of their resources.*

What if I were to brush off the opening question with a smile and 'Oh, it's not as bad as all that—how are you doing?', then enter into some Discovery? I could find out a little about my colleague's state of mind, political situation, current pressures, etc. before making any requests. Then, when the conversation returns to my reason for calling the meeting, since I am reasonably up to date with my colleague's situation, I would be much better able to frame my request and move the conversation towards a good solution.

There is nothing dishonest or manipulative about this approach, since my intention is to work openly with my colleague to find a solution that suits both of us. However, I also want to waste as little time as possible on unproductive discussion. Discovery helps me to avoid conversation barriers that an excessively direct approach might create.

them to launch into their prepared talks. A couple more questions from me and even more information was forthcoming. Some of the exhibitors remembered to ask me about what I did, and most requested a visiting card, but the flow of data was heavily in my favour.

This experience clearly illustrates that *to stay in control of a conversation I must favour listening over talking as much as possible.* It is the person who is listening most, and directing the conversation with their questions, who has most influence on the direction that the discussion takes. In particular, this person can move the conversation through a process of Learning then Guiding Discovery.

Last but not least, *Discovery will help me to optimise the delivery of any arguments or presentations that I intend to give*. It may even deter me from giving them at all. If, for example, I discover that my client is reeling from the consequences of a company reorganisation, then I will probably defer the presentation of ideas about our long-term relationship until a better time. While it may be disappointing to shelve work that I have taken a lot of trouble to prepare, it could be better to do this than to irritate or confuse my client with something inappropriate at that moment.

Learning Discovery and its Challenges

It helps to make a distinction between Learning and Guiding Discovery. Learning Discovery allows me to get facts and figures about projects, data about a client company's internal organisation, market statistics, and so on. Guiding Discovery, on the other hand, concentrates on the problems that the situation poses for the client and the needs that they have as a result (see the next chapter). This chapter focuses on Learning Discovery.

With reference to the Encounter Process, discussed in Chapter 2, Learning Discovery starts with the identification of Discovery targets—i.e. the things that I want to find out—during the Prepare step. However, such preparation can't guarantee sufficient coverage of the subjects worth addressing. This is because it is hard to anticipate all the topics that might lead to useful discussion, and because the dynamic of the client conversation can't be predicted.

There are occasions when clients' circumstances seem so complex that it is hard to know which points to focus on. Their projects are technically complicated, they are widely geographically distributed, they depend for their success on the evolution of international technical standards, they are working in consortia with companies that they usually consider to be competitors, the politics within their own organisations are intricate, etc. When faced with such bewildering complexity, it is crucial not to overlook something that could later turn out to be important.

In conversations with clients, I'm going to have to accommodate unforeseen topics. Indeed, I must facilitate this process by moving the conversation on, so that it doesn't get stuck on one particular subject at the expense of others. I may also have to help my client to develop the scope of the conversation. As we come to better understand some of the issues, completely new ideas may pop up. They may not be clear at first and I may even have to help my client clarify their thoughts.

The potential for confusion can be counterbalanced by imposing some structure, both on the conversation and on the data arising from it. This will help me to navigate around the issues that must be discussed, remembering what has been covered and what has yet to be addressed, and it may also allow me to assist my client's attempts to explain their situation.

DISCOVER-Y is a tool that provides such a structure.

DISCOVER-Y

DISCOVER-Y (pronounced 'discover why') is derived from a coaching tool[7] developed by Vincent Lenhardt for coaching individuals who seek to improve some aspect of their personal or professional lives. Not surprisingly this is useful to Customer-Facing Engineers, since many aspects of conducting a client conversation are similar to coaching. In particular, it is essential for a coach to develop a holistic view of the client's situation, and not to focus too quickly on just one aspect. Further, a coach has to be aware of their own natural tendencies (their comfort zones and also the subjects that they shy away from), and they must compensate appropriately. A coach also needs the ability to clarify situations that were formerly obscure, to allow their clients to see things in a new light and to enable them to make new decisions.

---

[7] See the '8 intervention zones' coaching tool in Vincent Lenhardt's *Coaching for Meaning* (Lenhardt 2004).

Basics

DISCOVER-Y can be used to:

- Identify Discovery targets before an encounter
- Identify new areas for exploration while in conversation
- Move the conversation on when it gets stuck on a topic
- Work with clients to visualise a situation
- Debrief to colleagues after an encounter.

The tool consists of a 'Y' on its side, and is essentially a Mind Map skeleton (see the diagram below). I am at the left-hand end of the Y, and my client is at the centre. Strictly speaking, the 'Me' node represents everyone from my organisation *at the encounter*, while the 'client' node represents the people *at the encounter* from the client organisation.

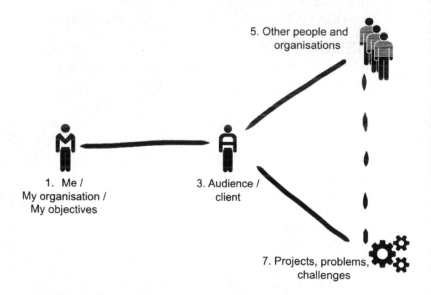

5. Other people and organisations

1. Me /
My organisation /
My objectives

3. Audience /
client

7. Projects, problems, challenges

Above and to the right of my client are the people and organisations that they are linked to (the 'who' of the situation). Below and to the right of my client are their problems, projects, technical ideas and challenges (the 'what'). That makes four nodes, which we call the 'odd zones', since they are labelled with odd numbers. The lines joining them are the 'even zones', representing the relationships between my client and the other zones and, in the case of zone 6, the relationship of other people and organisations with the projects etc. Since this is a Mind Map, we are free to draw other internodal relationships, and to add nodes.

The items to place in each of the odd zones will emerge during the course of a Discovery session, as will be described below. The easiest to imagine are the zone 7 items ('what'), which are typically the products and projects being discussed. Having identified items I proceed to ask for information about them, of course, and so I accumulate a list of knowns and unknowns about each of them.

As mentioned, the even zones capture the relationships between the objects in the odd zones: e.g. what I know about my client belongs to zone 3, whereas what I know about my client's relationship with my competitors belongs to zone 4.

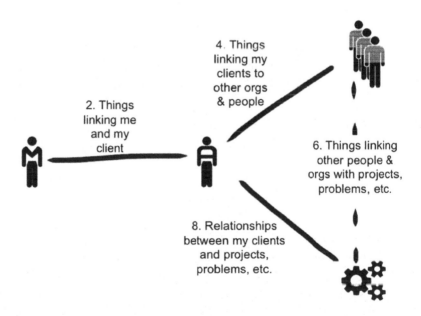

Zone 1 is special, since it represents me and my organisation. Hence, instead of thinking of things to ask about this node I prepare answers for questions that I anticipate my client will ask.

In doing this, I can imagine two branches of the DISCOVER-Y diagram that go off to the left, mirroring zone 5: 'who' and zone 7: 'what'. These are not usually drawn, since the DISCOVER-Y tool is oriented towards the client's situation, but it is worth remembering that, logically speaking, they should exist.

An Exercise

The following exercise should help you to become familiar with DISCOVER-Y. You may either do it with pen and paper, or simply think it through in your head.

Part 1 (two to three minutes)

You are an engineer working for a small medical imaging company with responsibilities for technical support and technical marketing. A potential client tells you that they need an ultrasound scanner for use on the International Space Station. List the questions that you could ask them at an initial meeting.

Part 2 (two to three minutes)

Draw the DISCOVER-Y diagram, number the zones and complete zones 5 ('who') and 7 ('what') with the names of people, organisations, projects, products, as appropriate (zones 1 and 3 always represent the people in the meeting, called 'me' and 'the client' for simplicity).

Part 3 (two to three minutes)

Position the questions that you wrote in Part 1 in the appropriate zones, next to the names of the people, organisations, projects, etc. that they correspond to (e.g. by giving each question a letter and writing the letters in the zones).[8]

The Discovery work that is prepared in this exercise—aimed at factual information—will be familiar to the reader. In fact, this familiarity is one of the issues. When I introduce DISCOVER-Y to groups of engineers, we normally start by listing questions relevant to the type of example just described. When these questions are organised according to the eight zones on the diagram, we invariably find that zone 7 ('what') has far more

---

[8] Possible questions are listed in Annex 1.

items than any of the others. The result of the exercise changes if, for example, there are Salespeople in the room. They tend to ask more questions in zone 5 ('who'), such as 'Who is the project funded by?', 'Who is involved in the decision on which scanner to use?', or 'Which other suppliers are you talking to?'

The exercise on the opposite page, that you may have just performed, is not only to familiarise you with DISCOVER-Y, it may also help you see if your questioning favours certain zones at the expense of others. Does it?

To be sure that you have interpreted the use of each zone as intended, please refer to the example responses in Annex 1. Generally, the odd zones (1: 'me', 3: 'the client', 5: 'who' and 7: 'what') do not pose any difficulty. However, the even zones deserve a closer look.

Even Zones

I pay special attention to the even zones since, as an engineer, my natural inclination is for straightforward, factual Discovery, which mainly involves asking for information about the odd zones. In particular, I am likely to have a preference for zone 7—the 'what' zone (see the suggested responses in Annex 1 for confirmation of this). While it is true that zone 7 deserves attention, it can also be thought of as the engineer's 'comfort zone', with all the associated dangers!

So, let's not neglect the even zones, which give me insight into the client's view of the situation, starting with their *perceptions* of the items in zones 1: 'me', 5: 'who' and 7: 'what'. These perceptions do not necessarily match mine, as the diagram illustrates.

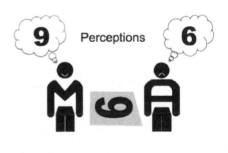

Based on these perceptions, the client probably has a number of *concerns*. For example, if they think that my scanner system has a quality rating of 6 stars, whereas they need a minimum of 8, then this would be a problem for them. Note that , since my perception

Concerns

of the quality rating is 9, I might easily overlook their concern if I did not discover their perception of the rating. Concerns therefore follow perceptions and they represent a second type of information to look out for in the even zones.

Finally, the client has certain *expectations* of me and my organisation (zone 2), of other people and organisations (zone 4) and of the projects, products, etc. that belong to this situation (zone 8). Pursuing the scanner system example, the client's expectations may incorporate some margin and so, rather than the minimum rating of 8, their expectation is for 10. Again, this is related to the previous pieces of information on the client's perceptions and concerns, but it cannot be

Expectations

deduced from them. It must be discovered through judicious questioning about the expectations themselves.

In summary, for the even zones, I must look out for:

CHECKLIST

- ❏ Perceptions
- ❏ Concerns
- ❏ Expectations.

Numbers were used in the above examples to clarify the meaning of these three factors, but it is rarely possible to be so precise. For example, if one of the items in zone 5 is my client's IT department, then zone 4 information could include my client's perceptions of the IT department (its power, competence, etc.), their concerns about the service it provides and their expectations for improvements. These are *qualitative* measures.

Notice that, since I feature on the DISCOVER-Y diagram in zone 1, my relationship with my client is represented by zone 2. The information associated with this zone can be particularly important—it includes the expectations that the client has of me and my organisation, and also their perception of our past performance.

Finally, Chapter 10 explains the use of a systemic approach for understanding complex organisations and situations, and this requires a good understanding of the relationships between the different parts of the system. In the DISCOVER-Y tool, this information is in the even zones, and the tool can therefore be used to support a systemic approach.

Use of DISCOVER-Y

For Encounter Preparation (with MAP)

DISCOVER-Y has two main uses during encounter preparation:

▸ The assessment of a situation (current knowledge)

▸ The identification of Discovery targets (info. to find).

It is used in conjunction with MAP, and is one of the tools used with its 'Plan' part. In fact, the 'My objectives' and 'Audience' parts of MAP can immediately be annotated on zones 1: 'me' and 3: 'the client' of the DISCOVER-Y diagram.

For encounter preparation, the diagram is drawn explicitly, then the different zones of the Y are annotated with information 'brainstorm style'. The Y diagram should be thought of as a basic Mind Map skeleton, and so I don't hesitate to add extra nodes and arcs as necessary. For example, if I have a direct relationship with one of the people or organisations listed in zone 5: 'who', I may draw an arc that represents it from zone 1 into the cluster of names at zone 5.

An example of the type of drawing that can be produced when using DISCOVER-Y for encounter preparation is given on the next page. In real life, this would be done on a wall chart, where there would be more room, coloured pens, and the participants would have the advantage of seeing information added to the diagram gradually. In order to clarify this one, I have added dotted lines around the items in the odd zones. The information associated with these zones is our objectives ('Get a meeting with Phil', etc.), and some data about Gizmo3 ('Intro'd 2012', etc.).

The other information on the diagram is about the relationship between nodes, and underline is used here to indicate where that information is missing. Specifically, we don't

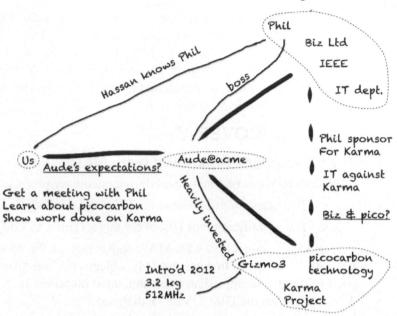

understand either Aude's expectations or Biz Ltd's capabilities in pico carbon technology. We do know that Phil is Aude's boss, that someone in our organisation called Hassan knows him, and that Aude has invested a lot of energy in Gizmo3. There is some additional relationship information in zone 6.

Imagine working on this type of representation with one or two colleagues, using a large drawing surface, coloured pens and plenty of coffee. The Y drives you to think of certain types of information, and provides a useful constraint to an otherwise freeform visual brainstorming process. The resulting picture is unlikely to be very elegant, but the process of producing it is invaluable.

From this point, I may go on to prepare slides that support the envisaged Discovery process. I would require material to help me address the points of interest just identified with DISCOVER-Y (e.g. roadmap slides to encourage a discussion of project timing, benchmark results to lead the conversation to key technical points, etc.), as well as slides that anticipate my client's questions and needs (i.e. collateral for zone 1: 'me'). Some techniques for organising this material—while maintaining a concise presentation style—are discussed in Chapter 7.

I finish this subsection on a warning note. Extensive preparation has a tendency to make me forget that my preliminary analysis of a situation is just that: preliminary. Armed with lots of data, ideas and slides, I may be tempted to share them with my client at the beginning of a meeting, instead of doing Discovery, as discussed.

Groundwork is important, but it is wasted if it leads me away from a listening posture. It should be used instead to reinforce that posture, helping me to ask the right questions, to quickly understand the responses and therefore direct the conversation accordingly. In this way, my preparation has enormous value, since it makes my real-time Discovery (i.e. the Discovery done in the client meeting) so much more effective.

In Real Time, During an Encounter

DISCOVER-Y is particularly powerful as a 'real-time' tool, for impromptu use in client meetings. In this case it stays either in my head or in my notebook but, in either case, it is used during the conversation itself.

When using the tool without notes I cannot, of course, accumulate detailed information about the different zones in the same way that I would with the support of paper. Rather, I refer mentally to the Y from time to time, especially if the conversation starts to get repetitive, becoming stuck in one zone. When this

happens, DISCOVER-Y reminds me to move the discussion towards zones that have not yet been explored.

As discussed, it is particularly important not to let zone 7: 'what' dominate either my thinking or the discussion with my client. This is an easy trap to fall into: not only is gravity pulling me down into this zone (the lowest on the diagram), but also, as an engineer, I may tend to focus on projects and problems more readily than on people (zone 5) and relationships (the even zones).

I must also remember to pay attention to zone 2. For example, I may ask for feedback on the last software patch that I sent the client, or on their perception of my level of service in general. In a pre-sales situation, it may be appropriate to simply ask 'Why us?', in order to find out if I or my company had been recommended by someone, or if the client came to me for some other reason.

It is also possible to use DISCOVER-Y in an open way with clients. A common practice in meetings is to use a whiteboard or flip chart to clarify ideas. Drawings can often communicate an idea more effectively than words, though sometimes it is difficult to know how to represent a complex situation in two dimensions. The DISCOVER-Y  diagram gives a handy starting point. If I feel that it would be a good idea to change the rhythm of a conversation by moving into drawing mode, I can sketch and explain the Y to my clients, add a few pieces of information and invite them to add more. Since the zones attract the full range of information that I am interested in, they guide our discussion in a helpful way.

As far as real-time use of DISCOVER-Y is concerned, that's it! Just like MAP and PAGE, the other 'routine' tools in the Toolkit, its brevity is one of its strengths.

As an Aid to Debrief

In a debrief situation, I can use the information I discovered during the client encounter to draw the Y diagram in advance of the discussion.

However, my experience is that once the Y diagram becomes densely populated with information and links, then the advantage of clarity that a sketch once offered starts to diminish. When this happens, the basic Y can be complemented with tables, charts and other representations. It may even be prepared in the form of slides or by using a Mind Map presentation program.[9]

The diagram on the next page shows a DISCOVER-Y chart that has been developed with a commercial Mind Map program. Some constraints are imposed by a book illustration—limited size and lack of colour, for example—but the essence of this technique is still apparent. I have chosen ovals for objects belonging to odd zones and rectangles with rounded corners for those in even zones. Data associated with objects in odd zones is contained in rectangles with right-angled corners. The picture shown is not completely expanded. If I were to click on the ⊕ symbols, then further branches and objects would be revealed. For example, my objectives, which appear in the rectangle to the bottom left of the picture, are not expanded. Neither is the information about the client (or Audience), Steve, which is represented by the rectangle towards the bottom of the picture.

Using a program, the amount of information that can be captured in this way is almost limitless, and it is easy to control which data is displayed at any one time. DISCOVER-Y has facilitated the organisation of this large quantity of information by providing the guiding principles for its structure. Without this, it would be easy to create a confusing rat's nest of data.

Mind Map programmes can export their data in many formats, including images, slide format and PDF. When a page-by-page or slide-by-slide presentation of information is desired, the table given below may provide inspiration on how to structure this. The table represents the same information as was captured in the Mind Map picture just discussed. It is divided into eight

---

[9] For an example of a free Mind Map program, see http://www.freeplane.org.

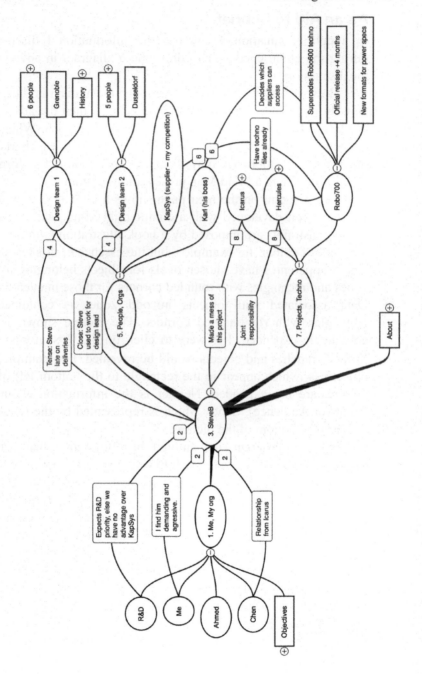

62

- Objectives: learn more about Hercules; access Robo700 files
- R&D, Ahmed, Chen
- Me

- Expects R&D priority
- I find him demanding/ aggressive
- Chen relationship (from Icarus project)

- Steve, snr engineer
- 5 years at Plexi
- Precise, workaholic

- Karl decides who accesses Robo700 tech data
- KapSys already have access!!

- Design team 1 (Gnb, data avail.)
- Design team 2 (Ddforf, ditto)
- KapSys (competitor)
- Karl (Steve's boss)

- Tension with design team 1 (S late on deliveries)
- Close to Design team 2 (S used to work for design lead)

- Icarus (failed project, data avail)
- Hercules (new project, ditto)
- Robo700 (techno, release in 4 months, new power formats, ...)

- S made a mess of Icarus project
- Joint resp. for Hercules
- H to use Robo700 tech.

sections, one for each zone of the DISCOVER-Y diagram. I could choose to keep all this information together in a single table, as in this example, or split the table into a number of separate pages or slides, as necessary. The benefit of the representation shown is that a link is maintained with the DISCOVER-Y spatial organisation of information through the pictograms that accompany each set of bullet points. Many people are helped by visual representations, and this tabular format is therefore a good compromise between traditional, textual lists and a complete two-dimensional picture.

On Listening

Simply Listen

Of course, there is no point in asking high-quality Learning Discovery questions if these are not followed by listening of the same calibre.

I consider myself to be listening effectively if:

▸ I really hear what's being said (I don't filter or interpret)

▸ The client feels the benefit of being heard (something like a sense of satisfaction or relief).

I regularly discuss the subject of effective listening in training classes, and participants quickly identify techniques that help, e.g:

☐ Use positive body language to encourage clients when they are speaking—eye contact, nods, etc.

☐ Take notes and ask for clarifications—these are not only useful, they show the client that you are listening.

☐ Use Playback—see the final subsection, below.

A corresponding blacklist of behaviours to avoid is useful too:

◼ Don't think about your next question

◼ Don't make premature judgements

◼ Don't get distracted by your own ideas

◼ Don't be anxious to suggest a solution

◼ Don't interrupt the other person—within reason.

A common mistake is to think of my next question when listening, and this is at the top of the blacklist. By letting my mind wander to my next question, I not only risk missing important information, I may also make my client feel that they are being subjected to an interrogation. Normal, agreeable conversation is littered with short pauses, allowing participants to consider what has been said and to formulate a response. If my questioning is too rapid and insufficiently linked to whatever my client has just said, then the dialogue seems unnatural, and this will be felt, consciously or subconsciously.

The last four bullets of the checklist can easily occur in the order given, like a series of inevitable mishaps leading to a catastrophe. Premature judgements are the result of my brain's desire to find cause-and-effect relationships in the data that it has to organise, but they are an obstacle to effective listening since, once I have 'explained' something that I am hearing, I stop listening further. Typically, I will go on to think of ideas that have been prompted by this new (premature and, perhaps, false) understanding in the quest to find a rapid solution to the issue being discussed. Impatient to share my insights, I may then be tempted to interrupt my client before they have finished talking ...

It is pointless trying to avoid these mistakes, since human beings are hardwired to make them. What I can do, however, is *use the checklist and blacklist to verify that my listening is effective.*

I suggest this because effective listening does not consist of a list of actions. The only action is to listen—that's it. I give my attention to the speaker and I let my listening apparatus take over. When listening goes wrong, it is usually because something in my brain has woken up and interfered with the listening process—typically judgements and wandering thoughts, as discussed.

Hence, the skill of effective listening depends on a good level of self-awareness: that is, the ability to simultaneously be present with my client, listening to what they are saying and, at the same time, being conscious of my own quality of listening. In this state, I quickly notice when I diverge from the 'dos and don'ts' checklists, and I take the necessary corrective action.

The second point on the checklist—take notes—is one way to take such action. When a new question or idea pops into my head, distracting me from listening, I *quickly scribble a note then return from the interrupt* and resume listening.

When I only have one brain to work with, the latter technique is probably my best option. If I am working with colleagues, however, then I have multiple brains at my disposal, and *it's good practice to agree on how questioning, listening and note-taking tasks will be shared.* Having backup from colleagues creates a great opportunity to simply listen.

Empathetic Listening

While the emphasis in this chapter is on Learning Discovery and on finding out data about a situation, I have already discussed the importance of ascertaining my client's Perceptions, Concerns and Expectations about different aspects of that situation. Empathetic listening is important when asking for this type of information, as it involves the client's emotions.

Since I use the term 'empathetic listening' several times in the rest of this chapter and the next, it is important to define it—not least because definitions of the word 'empathy' vary in the literature.[10]

Empathetic listening is the technique of using my own emotional apparatus in order to understand the feelings of my client. By using this technique, my level of understanding goes beyond a simple intellectual one. On the other hand, I stop short of sympathising with my client, which would imply mirroring their feelings, with the risk of being overtaken by them (which would impair my ability to think clearly).

Empathetic listening has two major advantages. First, it allows me to understand what really matters to a client. Second, the process of empathetic listening communicates to my client a deep comprehension of their situation, and this has a strong, positive effect on the relationship.

Empathy comes more naturally to some people than others, though we all have some capacity for it (this is not just a banal conviction—the neurosciences are beginning to uncover the mechanisms that allow humans and certain other animals to show empathy).[11] One thing is certain: the thinking process that I use

---

[10] I have found http://en.wikipedia.org/wiki/Empathy to be the most useful.

[11] See 'Mirror neurons' in David Rock, *Your Brain at Work* (Rock 2009).

when showing empathy is not at all like the one I use for scientific deduction. First of all, it requires an effort of imagination to put myself in someone else's shoes. Having done this, I assess what it feels like to be in this position—it is like thinking with the feeling part of the brain. This is why I included, in the definition of empathetic listening above, the phrase '... using my own emotional apparatus in order to understand the feelings of my client'.

While doing all this, I must keep a sufficient psychological distance from my client's feelings in order to be able to think independently (see my remarks on sympathy, below). To understand this last point, consider that I can listen empathetically *to myself*. To do this, I have to step back from my current situation, taking the stance of an observer looking back at myself. I can then listen to my own feelings empathetically, so that I am able to reason about them without letting the associated emotion take over. Again, this technique requires imagination and practice.

There are some common mistakes associated with empathetic listening. The first is to 'make it about me'. This can happen when, for example, a client describes a situation that I can easily recognise because something similar happened to me in the past. If I 'make it about me', I say something like, 'Oh yes, I know what you mean. Something similar happened to me last week. I'd just finished servicing my Bugatti when ...' Very irritating, with the opposite effect to the one that empathetic listening produces.

This is not to say that recognising a situation from my own history is a bad thing. However, rather than turn it into an anecdote about me, I can use it silently as I try to empathise with my client. For example, suppose my client just installed their accelerator board into their customer's PC, which promptly burst into flames. This setback reminds me of the time that I plugged a programmed microcontroller into an expensive, experimental GPS set, with similar, catastrophic results. Rather than saying, 'I know what you mean. When I was working for ...', I would do better to remember how I felt at the time (a mixture of astonishment, embarrassment and amusement), then probe my client to see if they feel something similar with respect to their case. Since I do not mention my experience at all, the client remains the centre of attention and they may be pleased to receive the understanding that I can show.

Another mistake is to confuse projection or sympathy with empathy.

Projection is the practice (and bad habit) of attributing motives or intentions to others based on my own feelings and biases. In contrast with empathy, which requires that I enter into my client's frame of reference, projection imposes my frame of reference on my client. When projecting, I assume something about someone else's feelings, based on my own experiences and biases.

For example, suppose my client avoids telling me anything about their experience with my competitor's products, even though they use them extensively. If I assume that this is because they favour my competitor as a supplier, this would be projection. What's more, if I assume that this is because my client has a strong code of ethics and would never talk to one supplier about another, then this would also be projection. In both cases, I make an assumption about the other person's motives or intentions, rather than finding out about them for sure.

The difference between sympathy and empathy is easily understood by anyone who knows about sympathetic vibration in physics: when I strike a tuning fork and put it on a wooden box next to another tuning fork, then the latter vibrates in sympathy with the first. Now, it is unlikely that the second tuning fork understands the emotional state of the first, so it is not empathising with it. Likewise, sympathy between people does not require an understanding of another's emotions, in the sense of being able to articulate an understanding of them. Rather, it is what happens when I actually come to feel the same way as my client. In a sense, it is when we share emotional energy (as opposed to mechanical energy, in the case of the tuning forks), and it is this sharing that consoles people who receive sympathy. In listening to clients, empathy is far more useful than sympathy since (1) it leads me to an understanding of their feelings that I can express, and (2) I do not become mixed up in the other's emotions.

Playback

Another essential technique for checking on the effectiveness of my listening is Playback.

Playback is the business of rephrasing what a client has said in order to confirm that I have understood, and to demonstrate that I have been listening. It provides a stabilising feedback path for the conversation.

There are two possible outcomes of Playback—I am right or I am wrong. Since both are good, I cannot lose! That is:

▸ If I have correctly understood what was said then I will know for sure that I've learned something, and I will have reassured my client that I am a worthwhile audience.

▸ If there is something wrong with my interpretation, then it will immediately get fixed. The client, assured that I am genuinely trying to understand, will help me.

Playback is quite straightforward when investigating the client's situation since the focus is on objective fact. For example, '... so, if I understand this correctly, 3% of our widgets were dead on arrival ...'.

However, Playback is not restricted to simply echoing raw data, and a particularly important application is for acknowledging a client's problems.

If a client expresses discontent with a certain aspect of my product or service, then they are telling me how they feel (a problem is subjective—the product or service in question may delight other clients). It then becomes important to demonstrate my understanding of my client's feelings since, if I do not, they are likely to become frustrated. Having taken the trouble to express their discontent, they will certainly want it to be acknowledged, and Playback allows me to do this. For example, 'I understand that three per cent of our widgets were dead on arrival' is inadequate Playback if a client is furious about this situation. It would be better to add, for example, '... and this failure rate is significantly below your expectations. You are therefore very concerned and you want to hear what we are going to do about it. Right?'

Playback can also be used to open up conversations that get stuck. Sometimes a client may present a situation as being closed, in the sense that there is nothing left to be said, but it is not in my interest to let the discussion finish on this note. For example, if I am trying to interest them in a new way of doing something, but they state flatly that their current methods work fine, then it might seem that there is nothing more to say. In these circumstances, it is important to acknowledge the client's statement, as it would be rude to simply ignore it and push an alternative view. Fortunately, a simple Playback device can open up the conversation again: using the word 'and'.

For example, 'I see that your existing design software is meeting your needs today ... *and*, given how the technology is evolving, what do you think is the next "big thing" that will lead you to update it?' or 'I understand that the fix is working well ... *and* what are your plans for maintaining it when there are operating system updates?'

The important points to note when using this device are (1) to use the word 'and' rather than 'but', since the latter can be seen as argumentative (D'Ansembourg 2007), and (2) to follow 'and' with an open question, rather than a closed one. A closed question would make it too easy for the client, who already seems to be trying to close off the conversation, to do so again. If, for the first example in the previous paragraph, I had said '... *and*, given how the technology is evolving, how long do you expect this to continue?', my client could simply reply 'About 10 years'—not a great invitation to further discussion!

Of course, we should not get too hung up on the use of one single word: there are alternatives to 'and'. With this in mind, I guess that you are ready to finish this chapter *so*, now that we have covered the simplest three tools in the Toolkit, what are you expecting next?

In Brief

✦ The Do phase of the Encounter Process should invariably start with Discovery.

✦ Learning Discovery is for finding out information about a situation.

✦ The DISCOVER-Y tool can be used to:

- Identify Discovery targets before an encounter
- Identify new areas for exploration while in conversation
- Move the conversation on when it gets stuck on a topic
- Work with my client to visualise a situation
- Debrief to colleagues after an encounter.

✦ The odd zones in a DISCOVER-Y diagram contain people and things, and even zones describe the relationships between them.

✦ To identify even zone relationships, I consider the client's:

- Perceptions
- Concerns
- Expectations.

✦ High-quality listening complements Discovery, helping the listener to hear what is really said and producing a positive effect on the speaker.

✦ Empathetic listening is the technique of using my own emotional apparatus in order to understand the feelings of my client.

✦ I use Playback of facts and feelings in conjunction with effective listening to confirm that I have understood, and to demonstrate that I have been listening.

DISCOVER-Y

For visualising discovery questions (a Mind Map)

Use in Prepare and Do to improve questioning coverage. Also for debrief.

Follow Up
Check
Do
Engage
Prepare

Y
discover

71

6. Guiding: SUBROUTINE

'The art of persuasion consists as much in that of agreeing as in that of convincing, so much more are men governed by caprice than by reason!',[12] Blaise Pascal, *Pensées*

'Ask for what you want and be prepared to get it',
Maya Angelou

Raising the Stakes

The preceding chapters describe *efficient* encounter methods that lead to a good *understanding* of the client's situation. This chapter raises the stakes and sets the tone for the remainder of the book. It recommends ways to have more *effective* encounters, allowing me to *influence* my clients' decisions.

Efficiency is related to effectiveness, and both are desirable: climbing a ladder efficiently will get me to the top quickly and this can be effective if the ladder is against the right wall and I know what I want on the other side!

Similarly, I can plan and run multiple client encounters with extreme efficiency, collecting extensive information and building strong relationships, but, for this to be worth doing, I must bear in mind the benefit that I seek (for myself and my organisation). Once this is clear, I need the ability to influence my clients, to ask them for what I want and to confront them when necessary. I chose the above quotations for this chapter as they hint at the complexity of this task.

In this chapter, I will introduce an extremely powerful approach to communication that takes me beyond the limits of Learning Discovery. As discussed, the latter technique gives an objective assessment of a situation—it is excellent for gathering factual information, and it can also give me clues about the relationships within a system. To go further, I need to understand how the situation *affects* my client and what they *need and want*.

---

[12] Original text: L'art de persuader consiste autant en celui d'agréer qu'en celui de convaincre, tant les hommes se gouvernent plus par caprice que par raison.

Based on this, I would like to influence what they decide to do—
i.e. the *solutions* that they adopt.

Guiding Discovery

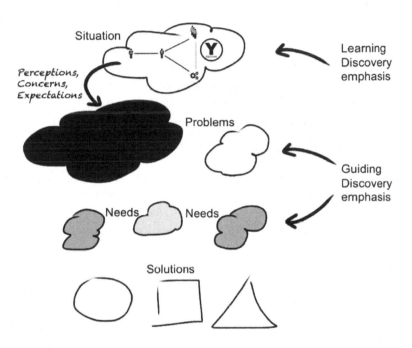

The diagram above introduces four important components of the
client conversation—the Situation, the Problems seen by the
client, their related Needs and the associated Solutions. The ability
to clearly distinguish these four components is tremendously
valuable in client conversations. It allows me to quickly step back
from the proceedings and understand its essential characteristics.
The components are defined as follows[13]:

> ▸ **Situation:** *Objective* information related to a topic.
> Independent observers should agree on the Situation's
> description, hence it should be free of judgements,

---

[13] The terms Situation, Problems, Needs and Solutions are capitalised in the
context of Guiding Discovery and the SUBROUTINE. Outside of this chapter,
they are generally not capitalised.

interpretations and generalisations (e.g. 'the yield is fine' is subjective and therefore not acceptable; 'the yield is 98%' is objective and OK). This information may be quantitative or qualitative, and it may be easy or hard to find, depending on circumstances.

▸ **Problems:** Aspects of a Situation that are unsatisfactory. A Problem is a *subjective* phenomenon and is likely to involve people's *feelings* (e.g. if a client is angry about a 98% yield that is, in fact, technically adequate, then the Problem is their anger, not the yield).

▸ **Needs:** In this context, *satisfaction gaps* that must be filled in order to resolve a given Problem. Needs must be expressed at the *highest useful level of abstraction* in order to open up my thinking to as many Solutions as possible (e.g. 'The client's Need is a 1% yield improvement' is too obvious and low level to be useful in the example being followed; 'The client's Need is to regain confidence in our ability to manage production costs' might be better).

▸ **Solutions:** *Concrete strategies* for fulfilling particular Needs. Note the common practice of suggesting a Solution as though it were a Need: e.g. when the client says 'We need to improve yield' they are really suggesting a Solution, not a Need.

As the preceding diagram shows, Learning Discovery is mainly concerned with the Situation component. It does, however, feed into Guiding Discovery by providing initial information on the Problems seen by a client. As discussed in the preceding chapter, investigation of the relationships between the client and their environment, as depicted in the DISCOVER-Y diagram, can reveal their Perceptions of their Situation and their related Concerns and Expectations. Very often, however, such an initial investigation will only reveal what Neil Rackham calls 'implied needs' (Rackham 1988). That is, needs that are really Solutions (as defined above), and which are somewhat shallow and obvious. In the case of trivial Situations where the implied need is synonymous with a simple and correct Solution—such as a part number, a replacement gasket or a software licence update—this

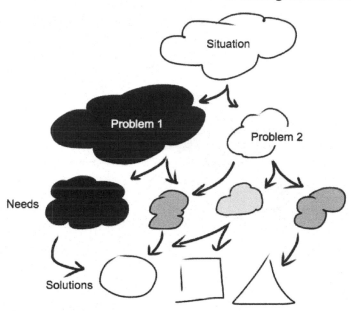

can be enough. However, in Situations where a Customer-Facing Engineer might really be able to add value, it is necessary to go deeper.

For example, in the sketch above, the top cloud illustrates a Situation that, upon investigation, turns out to harbour two Problems, one much larger and more ominous than the other. These are found to correspond to four different Needs (one of which is common to the two Problems). Three alternative Solutions are finally identified, but none of them will resolve all of the Needs. Both circles and triangles are needed.

However if, as shown in the sketch on the next page, I had jumped at the first Solution suggested by the Situation's description (i.e. the implied need—triangles), then I could have completely missed the necessity of circles!

Having leapt into a discussion of a particular Solution (triangles, in this case), I would be stuck with defending, for example, a particular feature of my triangle or struggling to bend it to fit Problems and Needs that start to come up in discussion.

Guiding Discovery is about investigating the Problems and Needs components of a scenario sufficiently well to (1) arrive at

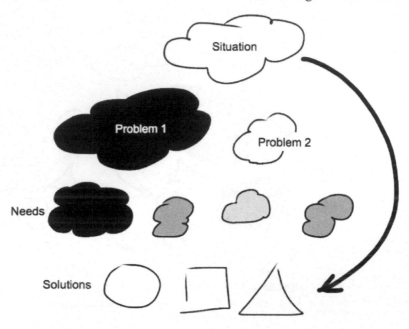

practical and adequate Solutions, and (2) where appropriate, clarify the value to the client of my contribution to these Solutions. By maintaining the conversation at the level of Problems and Needs for as long as possible, I both open up the discussion to Solutions that might not otherwise have been considered and allow the value of these Solutions to be fully understood. The latter point deserves some attention.

Imagine that I go to the doctor suffering from backache, headaches and lack of sleep. I feel terrible. The doctor takes a good look at me as I enter their office, asks a couple of questions and writes a prescription for some heel supports to insert in my shoes. This process takes about five minutes and, although I am sceptical as I leave the office, the heel supports do the trick and I am feeling much better within a few days. In the end, the cure was simple and did not cost much.

However, suppose the doctor were to take a little longer to develop and explain their diagnosis. Armed with a strong insight into the cause of my issues, they could check my symptoms—'Do you find it hard to sit for more than half an hour?', 'Does it hurt when you laugh?', etc. Although they might be tempted to rush this process, finding my responses predictable, the more care that they take, the more impressed I am by their empathy (i.e. their apparent ability to read my mind). They could build up a holistic view of my case which not only confirms their original diagnosis, but also leads them to find out if anything else is wrong. This patient approach makes me feel much better about paying their fee —i.e. I value their service more.

It is easy to see that this approach is equally important for Customer-Facing Engineers—their clients have Problems with their hardware and software, rather than their bodies, but the same principles apply.

Due process not only helps me to avoid oversights, it also lets the value of my intervention become more apparent. And, for my business to thrive, it is essential that my services are understood and appreciated. In fact, for my business to even exist, it has to make a profit; to make a profit, I have to have satisfied clients; and to have satisfied clients, I have to make them aware of the value that I am providing. Just doing a good job is not enough!!

Hence, Guiding Discovery has existential importance.

Its nemesis is the tendency to jump too early to a discussion or a decision about Solutions. This error is extremely common, and I call it the Short Circuit.

The Short Circuit

The Situation–Solution Short Circuit is an entirely natural phenomenon although, given the trouble it causes, it is surprising that evolution has not eliminated it from our DNA by now. Many intractable disputes—in the playground, the workplace and the geopolitical arena—can be explained by this tendency.

A Short Circuit is a direct jump to the end of a process without executing the intermediate steps. The cause of this jump is usually a combination of time pressure and impatience, leading to an excessive focus on one's ultimate objective … at the expense of the appropriate process for reaching that objective. The approach taken is therefore direct and often counterproductive.

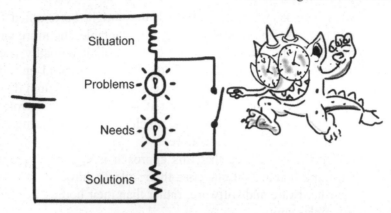

It is an easy mistake to make. Technical training and work generate vast quantities of hard information, and the mastery of facts, figures and procedures is at the heart of the CFE role. When given the chance, a natural reflex is therefore to present and explain things. In particular, it is hard to resist the urge to suggest Solutions once they start to become clear. Having listened for just long enough to deduce what might be needed, Customer-Facing Engineers might hear themselves saying, 'But that's because ...'; 'I'm sure it was caused by ...'; 'Let me explain how it works ...'; 'I've got a presentation ...'; and so on. When I hear myself using these words too early in an encounter, I know that my Hurry Monster is back and that I have made a Situation–Solution Short Circuit.

Mike short circuits

Mike meets Aude and starts their conversation by asking her about some issues that she has. Fine so far—he has started with Discovery. However, as soon as Aude says something that gives Mike an idea for resolving her Problem, **he makes a Short Circuit** and suggests his idea. Aude counters with 'Yes, but ...'. Mike insists, bringing strong, logical arguments to bear. The conversation gets stuck on the pros and cons of this one Solution at the expense of many other topics that might have been discussed.

I can also detect a Short Circuit by listening to my client's reaction, which, typically, is resistance. It is characterised by the words 'Yes, but …'.

Another method for detecting a Short Circuit is to check the blacklist introduced in the previous chapter and reproduced below. If I am contravening any of the following rules, then I am well on the way to making a Short Circuit:

- Don't think about your next question
- Don't make premature judgements
- Don't get distracted by your own ideas
- Don't be anxious to suggest a Solution
- Don't interrupt the other person—within reason.

Short Circuits are also often made by clients. For example, when a client says something like, 'Our yield is too low—we need an inspection camera with higher resolution', then they are making a direct jump from a description of the Situation (yield too low) to a Solution (a camera with higher resolution).

Guiding Discovery allows me to avoid Short Circuits and to recover from them, since it involves spending time on Problems and Needs. It is necessary when there is any doubt at all about these items and, at first, it is best to assume that this doubt exists. With experience, I come to recognise Situations where a Short Circuit is permissible but, since it is much more common to see inadvertent Short Circuits than unnecessary Guiding Discovery, we will ignore these cases for now.

When compared to Learning Discovery, a major challenge for Guiding Discovery is that it is far less clear what I am looking for. I cannot proceed on the basis of covering as many Discovery targets as possible when performing Guiding Discovery. Rather, topics of conversation will be suggested by the client's responses to initial questions, and we proceed from there. The structure of the conversation will also differ from that for Learning Discovery. While the latter mainly involves question–answer sequences, Guiding Discovery requires many others, and particularly suggestions followed by feedback.

For these reasons, the tool that I propose for Guiding Discovery—the SUBROUTINE—is particularly flexible. It can be employed in many different circumstances and will also make an appearance in Chapter 8, Challenging and Negotiating.

Guiding Discovery for a safety-critical system

My client asks me to supply a product that will fit into a safety-critical system. It is not clear why they have made this request at such a late stage in their design cycle.

If, having done some Learning Discovery, I immediately suggest that our Widget38 is a candidate for the application described, the discussion would probably then focus on the merits of Widget38, its feature list, its availability, its price, etc. Certainly, the client may be happy to let the conversation go this way—after all, they are the one that set up the Situation–Solution Short Circuit trap. However, we will probably quickly get bogged down in a discussion of technical and commercial obstacles.

Instead of transitioning from Learning Discovery to suggesting Widget38, I would do better to go to Guiding Discovery:

'Your project seems to be quite advanced. May I ask why the need for this product has only just been identified?'

'In fact, we were relying on a local university to develop this part, and they let us down at the last moment.'

'And so your biggest problem is now to finish on time?'

'That's one issue.'

'And the other is the performance of the system?'

'Even that isn't my worst headache. It's more that, with the university, we incorporated some original design features into this project, and it's going to be embarrassing if we can't deliver them.'

'Ah. So could we talk a bit about the main things that you need to demonstrate with this system?'

'Sure ...'

This conversation sequence illustrates the unexpected turns that a discussion can make if I take the time to discover more about Problems and Needs. Of course, this has to be directed towards areas where I can add value, and that is where the word 'Guiding' comes from. However, it can be appreciated that, at first, it may not be clear *precisely* where my Guiding Discovery is leading, even to me.

The SUBROUTINE

The SUBROUTINE tool consists of the Situation–Problems–Needs–Solutions process used in three different ways: as a Status Check, an Input Routine and an Output Routine. Its use model is shown below, with me on the left and my client on the right.

Process variant 1, the Status Check, is for me to use in order to assess what I am seeing and feeling with respect to the case in hand. Variant 2, the Input Routine, represents the flow for me to use when questioning and listening to my client, in order to understand their view of things. I use the third variant, the Output Routine, when I express myself to my client.

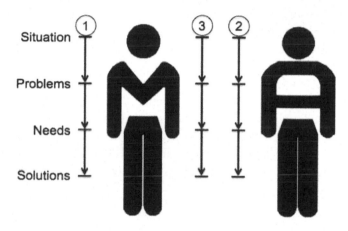

The three SUBROUTINE variants may be compared to a multimode subroutine. The tool is used in different ways throughout an encounter, just as a subroutine is called with different arguments from multiple locations within a computer program. Just as the availability of powerful subroutines can transform a software project, so the SUBROUTINE tool can transform client conversations. It requires practice, but the rewards are very significant— not because the SUBROUTINE is revolutionary, but because it captures certain fundamentals in an economical, engineering-style model.[14] Like the formula *voltage=current×resistance*, once understood, it's hard to forget.

---

[14] I explain the tool's origins at the end of this chapter.

In principle, I use the SUBROUTINE in the order given above: first for self-assessment; then for questioning my client; then for expressing myself. In practice, the way in which the SUBROUTINE is used will depend on circumstances rather than on this theoretical order.

Returning to the diagram above, it can be seen that 'Situation' is aligned with the head. This is because a Situation is something that I *observe,* as dispassionately as possible. In this context, it is important that a Situation be described in a factual way, using quantitative terms where possible. Problems, on the other hand, are subjective (the same Situation may be a Problem for me but not for someone else). They are therefore aligned with the heart, to represent feelings. 'Needs' are aligned with the gut, the home of hunger and appetite. Finally, 'Solutions' are associated with the legs since they imply actions, and legs give us movement.

Guiding Discovery uses all three variants of the SUBROUTINE, though the Input Routine (variant #2) is the dominant one. For this variant, the focus is on Problems and Needs, since the Situation is the domain of Learning Discovery and, as we have seen, the Solutions step is to be put off as long as possible. With this in mind and before discussing how the SUBROUTINE can be used, let's return briefly to Short Circuits.

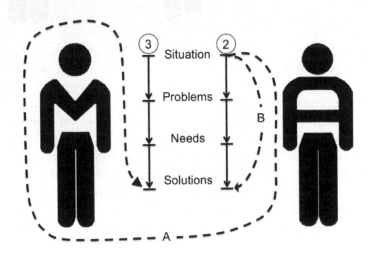

The first Short Circuit, shown as path 'A' on the diagram, is from the step of listening to the client's Situation to expressing a Solution. This is a pretty serious Short Circuit: six process steps have been skipped (discovering the client's Problems, Needs and attempted Solutions and expressing my understanding of the Situation, Problems and Needs). For example:

▸ Aude: 'I've got an issue with the buffering software.'

▸ Mike: 'No problem! I've got a script that can help ...'

Short Circuit 'B' is entirely on the client side. It is from the step of listening to the client's Situation to that of listening to their Solutions. This is the case where the client accompanies their description of a problematic Situation with a request for a specific Solution. For example:

▸ Aude: 'I need a script to fix this buffering problem ...'

A common, institutional example of a client-side short circuit is the Request for Quotation (RFQs, also called Request for Tender, RFT, or Request for Proposal, RFP). Such procedures describe the required Solution in great detail, making it hard for potential suppliers to do Discovery of any sort.

There is no magic solution to this type of Short Circuit, but at least it can be predicted (since RFQs are typically issued by institutions such as the military and major public and private companies). Having a healthy network within the issuing institutions, so that I can do Discovery about new RFQs before they are published, is one way to deal with this.

I hope that these examples make the nature of Short Circuits clear to the reader. This would be a good start, since a person who can recognise this trap is less likely to fall into it and, if they do, is better able to get out again. In the latter case, the corrective action is to somehow take the conversation back to an exploration of the client's Problems and Needs. This brings our discussion back to the use of the SUBROUTINE tool, and to a description of each of its three process variants ...

The SUBROUTINE for Status Checks

It's important to have a broad view of the circumstances surrounding an encounter before engaging with the client. This view must not only cover facts and figures but also my feelings about the case, links to other experiences, and so on. I need to get a sense of clarity and control (over myself and the things within my control), and hence a feeling of calm preparedness.

Establishing such a view will enable me not only to guide the proceedings more effectively, but also to adapt my plans as the encounter proceeds. This is a key capability since, no matter how thorough the preparation, unexpected information, questions, comments and requests can always take an encounter off course.

For example, if a client unexpectedly asks how long it would take to provide them with a minor product customisation, implying that this should be done for free, my response might be quite different in the case where I have clarified my view and in one where I have not. In the latter case, my temptation may be to reply directly to the request and give my best estimate. If, however, I have already decided that this client is inclined to take advantage of my good nature and that, from the point of view of my organisation, it's important to assert our Need for payment for such services, then my response will be different. In fact, I may consider that my client is using the effect of surprise in order to get a concession from me (if they were, this would be an example of manipulation—see Chapter 8).

While the example above shows the value of pre-encounter preparation, sometimes I just have to deal with things as they come up. Fortunately, the SUBROUTINE can be used not only in the calm of the Preparation phase—for a pre-flight check—but also in-flight, when conversing with the client. Certainly it is not so easy to use in these circumstances, and expert use requires practice, but the benefits are considerable. Rather than relying on instincts alone, using the SUBROUTINE allows me to take a quick step back from the encounter and make a rational, thoughtful assessment. The more often I do this, the more skilled I become and the faster I am able to do it. This allows me to better exploit new opportunities as they come up in conversation and, crucially, to stand up for my interests and those of my organisation.

To illustrate these concepts, let's take the example of preparing for a difficult call with a client who I know is unhappy about my product or service.

Situation

I start by looking for the facts and separating objective reality from my filtered version of it. Filtering occurs when I decode events, rather than simply observing them. In particular, I must look out for and avoid the following filters (Kourilsky-Belliard 2008):

CHECKLIST

- ☐ Judgements
  - 'The client was very late …'
  - 'The tracking system is useless …'
  - 'It's important to …', etc.
- ☐ Interpretations
  - Deductions: '… and so it will work/won't work'
  - Projections: '… they think that …'
  - Assumptions: 'It's because …' (without proof)
- ☐ Generalisations
  - 'It must …', 'You can't …'
  - Use of 'always', 'never', 'all', 'none', etc.

Basically, a judgement attributes value, an interpretation makes cause and effect links and a generalisation (over)simplifies. They therefore pollute and distort my objective view by adding unconfirmed explanations and removing valuable information.

EXAMPLE

When preparing to call my unhappy client, the stuff that comes spontaneously to mind may include a jumble of dark thoughts: 'As always, the idiots have jumped in without reading my emails—they think that …'[15] I can't stop this mental outburst, but I must separate such thoughts from real observations, such as, 'This is the third bug report received from them this week', 'They have version 3.4 of the product', etc. In this way, I start building up a clear picture of the Situation and begin the process of ordering priorities and calming my mind.

Spotting filters (judgements, interpretations and generalisations) is a little like noticing a certain type of car on the street. As soon as I have, say, a Volkswagen Beetle myself, I start seeing them all over the place! Similarly, once I become sensitive to the judgements, interpretations and generalisations in my own stream of thought, I become aware of them in general conversation. Developing the ability to recognise these artefacts, which often clutter the path to a clear understanding of a Situation, is extremely beneficial.

Problems

Realising that all Problems are subjective, I ask myself what emotions the Situation is provoking. It is crucial to do this, since we are not simple calculating machines. My ability to reason is strongly affected by my emotional state and to make good decisions I have to be aware of that state.

In the current context, the emotions concerned are often disagreeable ones, though the process applies equally well to pleasant feelings. I try to listen to myself empathetically, using the techniques described towards the end of the previous chapter. This helps me to step back from the feelings that the Situation triggers. Simply realising that I am irritated, for example, can be enough to prevent irritation from clouding my judgement.

Returning to my example, I concentrate on how the upcoming call with the unhappy client is problematic for me.[16] For example,

---

[15] 'As always [generalisation], the idiots [judgement] have jumped in [judgement] without reading my emails [deduction]—they think that… [projection]'

[16] We will see, below, that the same process can be used to work out how the Situation is affecting my client, but first things first. At this stage, the fact that my client is reporting a problem is a part of the Situation, not the Problem.

I may be embarrassed by the issues, annoyed with the client or stressed by the interruption. Whatever the issue, it is important, in this second step of the process, to check how the Situation is affecting me.

Needs

Using my understanding of the perceived Situation and Problems, I now try to identify my 'satisfaction gaps'. This means my wants and desires, as well as any professional interests and requirements.

If, for example, my boss is hassling me about this client, my prime Need may be to protect myself from further hassle. On the other hand, perhaps this client is taking a lot of my time, but isn't important from a business point of view. My priority might then be to allow myself the time to focus on business-critical work.

I emphasised when defining Needs at the beginning of this chapter that they should be expressed *at the highest useful level of abstraction*. To achieve this, I must be careful not to confuse my Needs with the immediate demands of the client. When they say, 'I need this bug fixed now!', they are not expressing a Need in the sense defined here. As far as I am concerned, fixing the client's bug is one possible way to satisfy my Need to fulfil my support role. It is crucial to distinguish between Needs and Solutions.

Solutions

In the final step of the process, I consider what I can do now. The process of examining Problems and Needs has made it easier for me to come up with some alternatives, and it is not always necessary to choose between them immediately.

Returning to our example, let's say that my prime Need is to protect myself from my boss hassling me. When the Need is expressed in this way, several possible Solutions come to mind: I could confront my boss, explaining that their close attention to this case is causing me stress, and asking them to show confidence in me; I could try to reassure my boss by explaining what I intend to do for the client; I could simply fix the issues being raised by the client so that my boss no longer needs to hassle me. These Solutions are not mutually exclusive.

These alternatives would not have been so obvious if I had expressed the Need as, for example, 'I need to reassure my boss' or 'I need to get this client's issues fixed'. These two statements are further examples of strategies for meeting Needs, rather than Needs in themselves.

That's my boss sorted out! Now, the process of examining my Problems and Needs may also have led me to understand that I am irritated and need to protect my time. Perhaps I should put off my client call, do one or two other things, *and calm down a bit?* That way, I will be in better shape when I make the call—a sensible precaution, as I find it difficult to hide my real feelings sometimes. If my client were to detect 'you silly customer' undertones in my voice, it would not be good!

Comments on Variant 1: Status Check

Overall, the first variant of the SUBROUTINE, summarised in the diagram and table below, ensures that I listen to myself in an empathetic way, understanding the facts of the Situation, the emotions that result from it and my associated Needs. Having made this Status Check, I can then decide what to do.

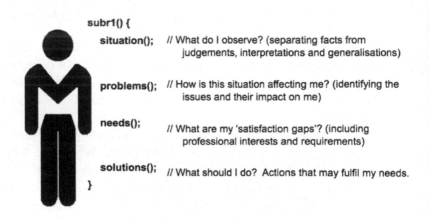

```
subr1() {
    situation();    // What do I observe? (separating facts from
                    //    judgements, interpretations and generalisations)

    problems();     // How is this situation affecting me? (identifying the
                    //    issues and their impact on me)

    needs();        // What are my 'satisfaction gaps'? (including
                    //    professional interests and requirements)

    solutions();    // What should I do?  Actions that may fulfil my needs.
}
```

The SUBROUTINE for Status Checks

Situation

I let everything related to the Situation come to mind—both objective reality (facts) and filtered reality (judgements, interpretations, generalisations). For example, 'The client was very late' is a judgement.

Once I have been through the above 'cleansing' procedure, I review the objective reality. What have I really seen and heard? For example, 'The client called in 10 minutes after the time agreed for the tele-meeting.'

Problems

Starting with the most obvious, I investigate the issues, listening to myself empathetically to understand how they are affecting me.

At the surface I may find, for example, that 'since the meeting started late, we didn't have time to get through the whole agenda'. Digging a little deeper will lead to, perhaps, a feeling of insecurity because I have the impression that I am not important to this client, or maybe to anger and irritation because I have a huge workload and can't afford to waste time.

Needs

Taking each Problem in turn, I try to identify the associated 'satisfaction gaps', or Needs.

I express my Needs at the highest useful level of abstraction possible, thereby creating the maximum number of Solution possibilities while avoiding the error of expressing Solution strategies at this stage.

Examples: If my Problem is a feeling of insecurity about a client, then my Need may be to understand their level of commitment to my company. If my Problem is that I am angry about wasting time, then maybe I need to feel more in control of my day. Behind this Need could be a deeper one, such as self-esteem—I feel bad about myself when events get out of my control. And so on.

Solutions

Very often, it is not necessary to go to this step straight away. Once I have understood my Needs sufficiently well, Solutions may be either obvious or non-urgent.

Each Need may have several alternative Solutions. I try to not become too attached to any particular one.

In the context of a negotiation, I identify my Fallback Solution at this stage (see Chapter 8).

The SUBROUTINE as an Input Routine

Having used the SUBROUTINE to clarify my view, the same four-step process can be applied for questioning and listening empathetically to my client—and therefore discovering their viewpoint.[17] I will continue with the same example—calling a client who has an issue.

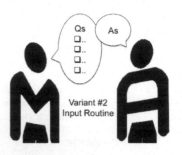

Variant #2
Input Routine

Situation

I question the client about the case, expecting to receive a mixture of factual and filtered information in their replies. That's OK— both may be useful, providing that I distinguish between them. For example, if my client protests '... the software is crashing all the time', I will register their annoyance, perhaps acknowledge it, and ask how often it has crashed this week.

Problems

While the exploration of a Situation is something that every Customer-Facing Engineer will be familiar with, the same cannot be said of the identification of Problems. For example, a client might say '... the software is crashing all the time and I need a new build today!'[18] When asked 'What is the problem?' a CFE might be forgiven for replying, 'The software is crashing'. But this is not the Problem: it's the Situation (similarly, 'a new build by today' is a Solution, not a Need).

The real Problem could be that the client is annoyed and feels like switching to a competitor, or that they are frightened of missing their deadlines and the resulting consequences, for example. What I am interested in is the impact of the Situation on my client and their organisation—how it affects them subjectively.

Of course, finding out about Problems is not as simple as asking a list of prepared questions, and the same applies to Needs.

---

[17] Please refer to the preceding chapter for a discussion of empathetic listening.

[18] This is another example of the Short Circuit.

To move the conversation forward, I may have to openly speculate about the client's Problems and Needs. This sounds risky, especially knowing that suggesting Solutions can generate resistance—why shouldn't the same thing happen when I am presumptuous enough to suggest to a client what their Problems and Needs might be?

But experience shows that, when I focus suggestions on Problems and Needs, clients tend to cooperate with me. *It's the opposite of what happens when I suggest Solutions prematurely.*

This is because of the intention behind my suggestions. I am putting ideas forward in order to help my client to articulate their views, so that I can understand them (rather than making suggestions with the intent of convincing them of something). Even if I make a few wrong guesses, my attempts to understand are likely to help my client to get their thoughts together, and hence I add value. Even if our conversation goes no further than this, it will have been a good use of my client's time, and they will appreciate my efforts.

Guiding with the SUBROUTINE

During Guiding Discovery, when investigating a client's Problems and Needs, it is quite acceptable to make suggestions. As discussed, this is not the case when at the Solutions step.

For example, if I say to a client, 'We could try running the processor at a different clock frequency …' then, whatever the merits of this suggestion, it will often be met with a defensive 'Yes, but …'. Alternatively, if my idea is accepted, the conversation is then likely to focus on how to implement this Solution, rather than considering others.

On the other hand, if I suggest to a client, 'It seems to me that your most urgent need is for raw processor speed—is that right?', they might confirm this or respond with, for example, 'That's important, but the speed of access to the cache is also a key …'. Whatever the response, it is likely that the conversation will continue to elaborate Needs *and it is unlikely that the client will object to me guiding their thoughts with my questions and suggestions.*

Needs

I now try to identify my client's 'satisfaction gaps'. If, for example, they are worried that their project will be delayed (Problem), then the associated Need could be for reassurance that I have the necessary skill and resources to help them reach their deadline. Or that, if they do miss the deadline, they will not be seen to be at fault. Or that, if they divert resources to fix the issues, then other projects will not suffer. Or that ... the Needs can be many and varied!

In using the SUBROUTINE, it is extremely important to distinguish Needs from Solutions and to appreciate the subjective nature of Problems and Needs. As far as my client is concerned, the real *value* of any Solution depends upon the Needs that it meets. The fulfilment of a Need is therefore associated with some sort of payoff for the client. For example, in case of a client in need of reassurance (just mentioned), fulfilling this Need could allow them to free up certain backup resources, perhaps using them for other valuable work. This is an attractive payoff, and putting it into words can make it easier for the client to recognise and confirm the Need itself.

It's safe to guess when using the SUBROUTINE

In general, people are willing to cooperate when I make suggestions about what their real Problems and Needs may be, since (1) this demonstrates a real interest in what affects them personally (remember that Problems and Needs, unlike Situations and Solutions, are subjective) and (2) this process helps them to better understand their Problems and Needs.

Hence, if I ask a client 'It seems really important for you that your team understands how the technology works—they don't really need to see a fully working product for some time. Is that right?', then, whether my guess is correct or not, my client is unlikely to object to the question. Further, the question has guided the conversation in a particular direction, avoiding any discussion of Solutions for the moment.

Solutions

Having ensured that I do not arrive at this step by means of a Short Circuit, what I am really interested in is *what Solutions my client has already tried.* A discussion of new Solutions may then ensue, but I'll get to that in a moment.

When this step is defined in terms of past Solutions, it can be seen that Short Circuits often skip this too! It is not uncommon to get trapped in a discussion of some new proposal, examining details of what is possible and letting enthusiasm for new ideas take over the conversation, before any check has been made on what has been tried before. For example, in the case of '... and I need a new build today!', above, it would be easy to reply, 'Well, I'm not sure that we can manage it today, because of the way that the build system works, but we could perhaps ...'. Rather than submit to this temptation, it would be better to review, however briefly, what has been tried before.

Comments on Variant 2: Input Routine

The Input Routine variant of the SUBROUTINE—for questioning and listening to my client—is the central pillar of Guiding Discovery. It is summarised in the diagram and table below. Its fundamental advantage is that it opens up a large range of possible Solutions and, in doing so, it *creates a collaborative working relationship* with the client. This contrasts with a simple customer–supplier or master–slave relationship that may result from a premature discussion of Solutions ('Hi Fred, nice to see

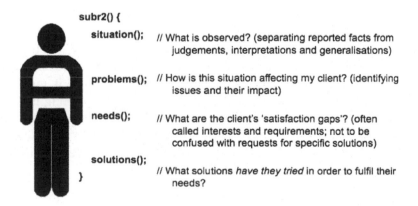

subr2() {

situation(); // What is observed? (separating reported facts from judgements, interpretations and generalisations)

problems(); // How is this situation affecting my client? (identifying issues and their impact)

needs(); // What are the client's 'satisfaction gaps'? (often called interests and requirements; not to be confused with requests for specific solutions)

solutions(); // What solutions *have they tried* in order to fulfil their needs?

}

you. I need some new widgets.'—'Sure. How many? What colour?'). By using Guiding Discovery, I can add real value both to the conversation and to the Solutions adopted as a result of it.

A possible Discovery obstacle is that my client may withhold or simply not have information that I seek. It could be that their Problems and Needs are not clear to them, or they may be unwilling to talk about them.

This disclosure issue can be encountered at any step of the four-step process and may be for cultural reasons—each country and company has its own tendencies in this respect—or because of specific circumstances (e.g. a company in the process of acquiring another will be subject to many legal constraints, a person embarrassed about a failed project may avoid talking about it, etc.). When this occurs, the first thing is to notice what is happening.

The obstacle may be simple to detect—for example, if my client tells me that certain data is confidential—or information could be discreetly concealed. In the second case, *I am far more likely to notice that information is being hidden if I adopt a Guiding Discovery approach*, rather than a simple Learning Discovery one. The latter can be likened to gathering mushrooms in a forest. It requires a keen eye and some ideas on where to look. However, I don't worry unduly when I fail to find mushrooms in a particular spot; I simply move on to the next. Guiding Discovery is more like a dog searching for truffles. It sniffs around a bit, gets a scent, then digs like crazy until the truffle is revealed!

When the issue is that my client, in spite of being willing, finds it hard to answer my questions, then Guiding Discovery, using the SUBROUTINE, is certainly the favoured approach. I would like to reiterate the point made earlier, that actively suggesting to my client what their Problems and Needs might be is not only acceptable, it is good practice. Though it may sound intrusive, it is much more helpful than hastily pushing new ideas and Solutions. Of course, to use this technique effectively, I must be able to distinguish between Problems, Needs and Solutions, and I hope that the many examples in this text are helpful in this regard.

The SUBROUTINE as an Input Routine

Situation

When listening to my client, I separate factual from filtered information.

It is useful to be able to spot filtering, since this provides me with a starting point for a sequence of questions. For example, I can discover what is behind a client's judgement that a device is 'slow' by asking, 'When you say "slow", do you mean less than 10MHz ...?'

Problems

I discover which aspects of the Situation are problematic for my client. It's OK to guess, e.g: '... and so if the sampling rate is below 10MHz, you will miss defects?'

Behind the obvious Problems may lie more interesting issues, linked to the way that the client feels about a past or present Situation, or to their expectations or fears for the future.

I use my experience of similar Situations to empathise with my client, avoiding the temptation to make it about me, e.g: I refrain from 'I had a problem like that once ...'.

Needs

Discovering Needs is *the* crucial step and, though it requires some skill, it is safe. If I demonstrate a genuine desire to find out what my client needs, they will usually help.

It is rare that people fully understand their Needs and they are therefore often open to suggestions. This is not the case for Solutions, where suggestions tend to be met with 'Yes, but ...' and other forms of objection.

To help someone understand the relative importance of Needs, I may discuss the payoff should they be met.

Solutions

I investigate the Solutions that my client has already tried.

A real conversation or negotiation will not follow a linear path through the SUBROUTINE process—it will jump around. I therefore need to be assertive in taking the discussion back to an earlier step when I see that Solutions are being discussed too early.

Beware: clients may push to go straight from a discussion of the Situation to their ideas for a Solution. This is one example of a Short Circuit.

The SUBROUTINE as an Output Routine

This is how I use the SUBROUTINE to express myself:

Situation

I start by describing, as best I can, the facts of the case—I present observations. This is a good starting point since (1) it serves to sync everyone up on their views of the Situation, and (2) it sets the tone of the conversation to one of agreement. The benefit of sticking to an objective presentation of the Situation is that any misunderstanding can be dealt with by an

Variant #3
Output Routine

investigation of the facts—likely to be far less controversial than an exchange of opinions, which would involve the comparison of my perception of the Situation (my filtered reality) with that of the client.

As always, care must be taken to distinguish facts from judgements, interpretations and generalisations. For example: 'The technicians have done a fantastic job restoring those three clapped-out engines. It's always difficult with such old technology ...', would be better expressed as, 'We are very pleased with the work of the technicians. They have restored the three engines much faster than we expected. The technology is from the 1960s and our experience is that ...'.

Note that opinions are expressed even in the second, improved version of the statement. However, these judgements are acceptable since the speaker takes ownership of them. What is important when expressing myself using the SUBROUTINE is, at each step, to avoid unnecessarily controversial statements. This does not mean avoiding issues. In fact, less controversial wording is often more accurate and honest, as in this case. Nobody can object to 'We are very pleased', but they can disagree with 'The technicians have done a fantastic job'.

Using the SUBROUTINE to wind up a Discovery session

Please note that the language of this example may sound artificial. This is simply because it is written in a textbook and the SUBROUTINE process is laid out step by step. In real life, I would use my own language and presentation style.

'We understand that you have moved into the commercial satellite business and are looking for a complete and cost-effective solution for a telescope imaging system. You are concerned that your current development and outsourcing arrangements are not suited to this market, which requires faster turnaround times than those that you are used to. You have tried working with one other subsystem supplier, but this was not successful' (*Situation—a playback of the client's Situation, Problem, Needs and attempted Solutions*).

'We are very happy that you have called us but concerned that we will not be able to meet your schedule expectations' (*Problem*).

'With this in mind, we believe it's important to get some experience of working together before embarking on such a large project. This would allow us to agree a more accurate, lower risk statement of work for your telescope imaging system' (*Needs*).

'Our first idea, that we would like to discuss, is to supply you with one of the smaller satellite subsystems, such as a camera. Please could you give us your reaction to this idea for such a relationship-building project and, if you agree with it, what you think of the satellite camera idea' (*Solutions*).

To appreciate how the discipline of the SUBROUTINE helps in this case, try modifying some of the text, breaking the rules about objective observation, taking ownership of feelings and opinions, making requests in the present, etc. For example, what is the effect if I say 'We are concerned about your schedule expectations'?

Very often, the Output Routine variant of the SUBROUTINE, for expressing myself, is used after a session of listening to my client and understanding their Situation, Problems, Needs and attempted Solutions. All four of these elements can now form a part of the Situation that I play back to my client at the start of the process. For example, if my client just explained to me that they are frightened of what might happen if their test engine were to overrun in the absence of trained personnel, and that they need a safety system that lets them sleep at night, then all of this forms part of the Situation as far as this process is concerned (even though, when listening, the information may have come out of the Situation, Problems and Needs steps). Typically, I would start a summary by saying, 'I understand that …', or 'You have told me that …'. Such a formulation is accurate and uncontroversial, as just discussed.

Problems

This step is used to express how the Situation affects me and my organisation and any interests, desires and wants that I have as a result. The word 'Problems' may not be the most appropriate in all circumstances, since there are many occasions where I have no negative feelings to report. How this plays out therefore depends on the reason for expressing myself.

In the context of Guiding Discovery, having used the SUBROUTINE's Status Check and Input Routine variants for listening empathetically to myself and my client, I may now be experiencing many different emotions. If the client has revealed a new project opportunity, I might feel enthusiasm, excitement or surprise. If they have been talking about a new product idea then I could be impressed, intrigued or dubious. If they are explaining some change in plans then I may be astonished, disappointed or even angry. Just a few examples to illustrate the wide range of possibilities.

It is not always necessary or wise to reveal one's emotional state, of course, but there are many occasions where it can be the right thing to do. If I really am enthusiastic about my client's project, then it is an excellent idea to let them know this. I should not assume or hope that they can work it out for themselves. On the other hand, if I feel that they are letting me down, manipulating me or indulging in some other vice, then I should probably confront them.

The key to doing so is to take ownership of whatever emotion is concerned. This simple trick allows me to express all sorts of feelings and to confront people about the most awkward subjects.

For example, if a client has just explained that the recent reorganisation in their company has left them without the budget to fulfil their earlier commitments to me, then I have the choice

9
EXAMPLE

between, 'But that's completely dishonest!' and 'I feel extremely disappointed by this—it had not occurred to me that your company would not honour this commitment.'

On a happier note, although 'Your project is fantastic' may be a positive thing to say, it is a completely judgemental statement, with all the drawbacks of this type of expression (it could be interpreted as approval and encouragement, for example, and if something goes wrong later ...). Better to say, 'Having listened to you describe the project, I feel really enthusiastic about it', which is, in fact, far more accurate.

The Output Routine variant of the SUBROUTINE can also be used outside of the Guiding Discovery context, notably for:

▶ Explaining something of a technical nature

▶ Promoting an idea, product or service

▶ Requesting help, resources or change.

The first case might occur when responding to a request for technical support. Sometimes, such interactions can be problematic and, having summarised the Situation in a factual way, the Problem step can be used to express whatever difficulty I perceive. If I'm worried, for example, that the quick-and-dirty fix being asked for will end up being adopted as a permanent solution and cause me a long-term support headache, then I can express my fear at this step.

 A final example, this time for requesting change (the third bullet point): if I am working in my client's offices for a few days and they have installed me at a desk near the coffee area then, indeed, they might be offended if I were to say, 'I can't get any work done because there is too much noise.' However, if I were to express the Problem as, 'I am finding it hard to concentrate as I am used to working in a very quiet environment', then it is almost impossible for anyone to take offence. By describing the impact on myself, rather than resorting to generalisations ('I can't get any work done') and judgements ('too much noise'), I am able to express myself with surprising candour.

It can be seen that, when I express feelings at this step, I use an approach consistent with that used for describing the Situation.

That is, without judgement, interpretation or generalisation and taking ownership of any feelings that I describe.

Using the SUBROUTINE to confront a client

Please note that the language of this example may sound artificial. In real life, I would use my own language and presentation style.

I supply Engine Control Units (ECUs) to a car manufacturer. They are working with a prototype, configuring it, testing it and comparing it with a similar system from my competition.

'I see that the fuel economy figures are 9% worse for our ECU than for the other system. However, on examining the readouts, I notice that seven warning messages were overridden during the configuration of the ECU. Also, I understand that a student engineer did this configuration work' (*Situation—objective observations*).

'When I learn that our ECU was configured by an inexperienced person, and that the results of the work are being unfavourably compared with those from a competitor product, I feel worried and, frankly, somewhat annoyed' (*Problems—taking ownership of my feelings, avoiding, for example, 'This is annoying!'*).

'I would like the chance to show you what our technology is capable of and to be assured that the trials do not handicap my company' (*Needs—at quite a high level of abstraction*).

'Please could you explain what you think happened here?' (*Solution—a request framed in the present*).

Needs

This step of the process is for expressing my Needs (if it is appropriate to describe my client's Problems and Needs, then it is done at the Situation step, as explained above). Hence, I arrive at this step when I have a Problem and I wish to obtain my client's cooperation in resolving it.

Once again, the challenge is to express myself in a way that is clear, honest and effective. And, once again, the technique is to speak in terms that my client cannot contest. This means *taking ownership of my Needs* and *describing them at the highest useful level of abstraction*. This is because (1) it is difficult for someone to argue about someone else's Needs—only their owner can really know what they are—and (2) a listener finds it easier to understand and relate to Needs that are expressed at a high level. We all share certain fundamental Needs and the higher the abstraction level, the closer we get to these fundamentals.

9
EXAMPLE

To take an extreme example, everyone can understand another person's Need for food and shelter—this is a basic Need or, looking at it another way, a Need expressed at a high level of abstraction. At a lower level, a person might say, 'I've got to keep my job', or 'We absolutely must finish the project this quarter.'

Another advantage of abstraction is that more abstract Needs are, by definition, further from specific solution strategies, and they therefore open up more alternative Solutions.

9
EXAMPLE

A technical example: suppose that my client's computer system has just crashed and they have lost five work days on a project that has to finish in two days (*Situation*). Given their resources, they estimate that they will now be at least 24 hours late with their delivery. This is worrying, to say the least (*Problem*). The primary Need is to find a way to bring the project in on time. Digging deeper, I might find secondary Needs: to recover certain files or to have 24/7 support, for example. However, each of these Needs may have multiple, alternative Solutions. It is therefore important to maintain the distinction between Needs and Solutions.

Solutions

This is the step that I am often itching to reach: where I propose a way forward, some next actions, a technical fix, etc.

There is no magic way to ensure the adoption of my Solution proposals at this step. The real work is done in the preceding ones. However, a couple of points are worthy of attention. When making a proposal I should:

▸ Provide alternatives

▸ Concentrate on the present.

I mentioned the importance of alternatives in the previous section. One of the advantages of exploring the Needs associated with a Situation is that many alternative approaches can be revealed. It is often the case that one of these will be obviously more advantageous than the others. Nevertheless, people do not like to feel cornered, and so the presentation of alternatives is a good way to make them feel comfortable with the choice that they make.

The second bullet point concerns an issue that is frequently neglected. When making proposals, my focus is often on the future. This is the nature of a proposal— it must be for something that has not happened yet. However, when I ask for agreement, if I invite actions that will happen in the future only, then I create difficulties both for my client and for myself.

For example, if I were to finish a presentation by saying, 'Do you think that this idea can be incorporated into your roadmap for next year?', then, if the client acquiesces, both they and I will have to follow up on this commitment. Sometimes there is no alternative—the nature of my request is that it requires a future commitment. However, on many occasions it is far simpler for everyone if I ask for something that can be realised straight away.

For example, I may ask my client for feedback on what I have just suggested, or I could ask them to explain their plans for something that featured in my presentation. This approach can, in fact, lead to stronger commitments for future action than direct requests. If I ask my client for feedback, then I leave them free to decide for themselves what they say and what they decide to do. It's possible that they are enthusiastic about my ideas, and they might suggest some future actions. If they make this suggestion spontaneously, without feeling that they have been obliged to do so, then their motivation to follow through will be much stronger than if I had extracted the commitment from them at the end of my presentation (JouleBeauvois 2002).

Comments on Variant 3: Output Routine

The SUBROUTINE for expressing myself to my client, summarised in the diagram and table below, is key to being able to deliver clear, complete messages, even when the content is potentially controversial.

I have described the use of the SUBROUTINE in the context of Guiding Discovery, but I hope that its usefulness in other Situations has also become apparent. As shown in the example on page 100, this third process is particularly helpful in circumstances where I have a tricky message to deliver and I am concerned about

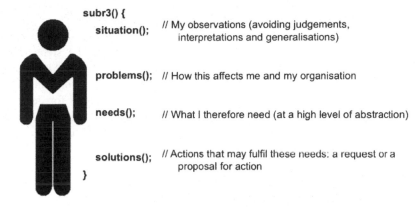

```
subr3() {
    situation();    // My observations (avoiding judgements,
                    //   interpretations and generalisations)

    problems();     // How this affects me and my organisation

    needs();        // What I therefore need (at a high level of abstraction)

    solutions();    // Actions that may fulfil these needs: a request or a
                    //   proposal for action
}
```

my client's potential reaction. In other words, the SUBROUTINE's third process is an excellent tool for confronting clients—it allows me to stand up for myself and my organisation with a reduced risk of provoking conflict.

A further example: if I am working at a customer's site to support their evaluation of our software and I find that my work is impossible in the prevailing conditions, then it is important that I ask them to make some changes. A somewhat thoughtless approach might be to say, 'Look, we're never going to be able to finish this work for you without some better workstations and support from your engineers.'

Using the SUBROUTINE in order to structure my request, I would say something like, 'As you can see, we're struggling: I've just emailed you a short report with the status and issues *(Situation)*. Long runtimes are slowing the work, as is our lack of knowledge of the design case *(Problem)*. To finish on time, we need to work in conditions that are closer to those of your engineers, with faster machines and an injection of design knowledge *(Need)*. Can you please explain why things are set up like this and anything you can do to help? *(Solution—a request for action)*.'

These examples will be familiar to anyone who has studied or practises Non-Violent Communication, and I encourage the reader to consult the web-based references for leads to further material on this subject.

The link to Non-Violent Communication

While the four-step SUBROUTINE process is extremely simple, it is hard to implement well. Hence, my practice of the steps is *more important than my intellectual understanding* of them. Although it is difficult, within the confines of a book, to go beyond intellectual understanding, there are plenty of resources available for developing one's skills in using the SUBROUTINE. The tool is essentially a condensed version of a number of existing techniques, and understanding its origins will therefore help the reader to find the useful, related resources.

The picture of a person in four parts comes from the literature on Non-Violent Communication (NVC). The outstanding contribution of NVC, in my view, is that it focuses on performing each of the four steps *properly*. The first difficulty is that this requires a larger active, non-judgemental vocabulary than most people possess. The majority of us often fall back on 'That was good/bad/lousy/great'—words that are essentially binary (and judgemental) in nature. However, the world is analogue and Situations, Problems and Needs must be expressed with more discernment if our communication is to be effective.

Books and courses on NVC abound, and they include exercises and tables of vocabulary for use in describing feelings (hence Problems) and Needs. All the words in these tables are easy to understand—hence they must be in my passive vocabulary. However, it is amazing how difficult it can be to describe Problems and Needs without recourse to the tables at first.

A second, major contribution of NVC is that it applies the four-step process in all three of the ways that I described above—first with its use for self-empathy, then for empathetic listening, then for expressing myself. Other systems that I have found, while being based on the same process, apply it to only one of the three ways.

The SUBROUTINE as an Output Routine

Situation

The Situation that I describe is usually based on the information gained from processes 1 and 2—empathetic listening to myself and my client.

I describe the Situation objectively, avoiding filtering (judgements, interpretations and generalisations).

If I wish to play back what I learned from my client using SUBROUTINE process 2 and Guiding Discovery, then it all goes here: I report the client's Situation, Problems, Needs and attempted Solutions as part of my Situation.

Problems

I express what is unsatisfactory (or, sometimes, satisfactory) in the Situation from my point of view.

It is not always necessary or advisable to reveal my emotional state, but it is important to know how to do so when the occasion justifies it.

I take ownership of whatever emotions are concerned. For example, 'When I hear that the project has been cancelled, I feel disappointed' is better (less judgemental and more accurate) than 'That's disappointing!'.

Needs

The Needs expressed should relate to the Problems previously described.

I describe my Needs using terms that refer to me only; e.g. 'I need to understand X better' rather than 'I need you to explain X to me more clearly'. The former cannot be disputed, but the latter may be seen as an accusation.

Needs should be described at the highest useful level of abstraction, leaving as much room as possible for alternative Solutions.

Solutions

I suggest a Solution or make a request for action, checking that I did not inadvertently jump to this step directly from the Situation one!

I frame my requests for action in the present, if possible. Asking for a promise of future action sets up a 'to do' on one side of a conversation and a need to check the action on the other. Better to ask someone to explain something immediately, or to play back their understanding of an issue, for example.

When requesting actions, I suggest alternatives where possible, in order to avoid giving the other person a feeling of being trapped.

In Brief

✦ Guiding Discovery allows me to understand how a Situation *affects* my client, and to develop our joint understanding of their *satisfaction gaps*.

✦ The enemy of Guiding Discovery is the Short Circuit: a premature jump to a discussion of Solutions. There are two main types: those that I make and those made by my client. I must avoid making the first and recover from the second.

✦ The SUBROUTINE tool supports Guiding Discovery and other communication tasks. It is based on a four-step process: Situation–Problems–Needs–Solutions.

✦ By focusing on Problems and Needs, I am able to guide the conversation much more easily than if Solutions are prematurely discussed—the latter Short Circuit error tends to produce resistance or devalue the conversation.

✦ There are three variants of the SUBROUTINE process: a Status Check, for self-empathy, an Input Routine, for questioning and listening to my client, and an Output Routine, for self-expression.

✦ In using the SUBROUTINE, it is important to recognise judgements, interpretations and generalisations. They are to be avoided in self-expression.

✦ When expressing feelings and opinions, I must take ownership of them. This allows me to tackle difficult issues with a substantially reduced risk of conflict.

✦ Requests for action should be framed in the present wherever possible.

✦ Guiding Discovery primarily uses the Input Routine variant of the SUBROUTINE, though all three variants are called on in a client conversation.

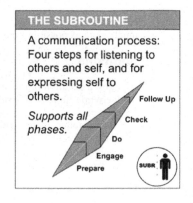

THE SUBROUTINE

A communication process: Four steps for listening to others and self, and for expressing self to others.

Supports all phases.

Follow Up
Check
Do
Engage
Prepare
SUBR

7. Presenting: TWO-MINUTE MESSAGE

'Power corrupts, and PowerPoint corrupts absolutely',
Edward Tufte

In his famous article 'PowerPoint is evil' (Tufte 2003), Tufte highlighted the dangers of over-reliance on presentation tools such as PowerPoint to convey information. However, in spite of Tufte's warnings, many people still use 'GPS' as their main tool for preparing meetings and presentations (GPS = Get **PowerPoint** Slides—see Chapter 3).

There is nothing wrong in using slides when preparing a meeting. However, I strongly believe that an excessive dependence on slides *to drive* client interactions is dangerous, for reasons which include:

▸ If I use a slide set to *drive* the conversation, rather than *support* it, then I will be locked into a linear, 'one thing after another' presentation flow. This reduces flexibility. In the worst case, I will fall into the trap of reading what is on my slides.

▸ There is a tendency to reuse old slides to gain time when preparing presentations. However, the value of a set of slides depends upon whether it suits my immediate objectives and audience. Old slides will not necessarily be suitable in new circumstances.

▸ Some slides can be visually very attractive. If I start my preparation by looking at past presentations—in other words, if I let existing slides dominate my thinking—then I will tend to include attractive slides that are not really useful. The result may be confusing, over-long, or both.

In spite of these dangers, for practical reasons, I use and reuse slides on a daily basis. What I really need, therefore, is a method for producing high-quality presentations, quickly, only using existing material where it makes sense. I need to do this in a way that puts me in control of my presentation, using slide support as appropriate, but not excessively.

Slide fatigue is common, and I often hear a sigh of relief when I turn off the projector. Many clients appreciate the chance for simpler, more direct interaction. Further, if I do need extra support for my arguments, there are various alternatives: flip charts, demonstrations, physical models, metaphor, and so on.

The ability to have an effective client interaction without slide support is also important on occasions where it isn't possible to use slides. Some organisations—military institutions and advanced research laboratories for example—don't allow visitors to enter with laptops, pads or phones. And there are always those occasions where the slide projector breaks down.

The Right Way to Prepare a Presentation

First, I throw away the GPS and go back to my MAP. This means, as discussed in Chapter 3, starting with 'My objectives' and 'Audience'.

Based on this solid foundation, I now do something rather counter-intuitive. Disregarding the entire accumulated knowledge of humankind, including the slides that I created last week, I take a blank piece of paper and write down a synopsis of what I will present. I endeavour to write full sentences, rather than bullet points, since full sentences catch ideas more completely. I want these ideas to be clear when I come back to them later. This is the first part of my Plan.

To reiterate: I don't look at any existing PowerPoint, web pages, books, fortune cookies or other sources of wisdom. If I were to do any of those, then my thoughts would inevitably be influenced in some way. By starting the planning step 'blindfold', I put myself in a position to capture my own, original ideas, however modest. I am then able to select from existing material in a way that supports these ideas.

Perhaps I will find, when I check on what's out there, that I've forgotten something important, or that my first thoughts were nonsense! That doesn't matter, so long as I give myself a chance to think independently at the start of the process.

Creating this synopsis may not take long. When people talk about capturing their ideas on the back of an envelope, or on a napkin, they are describing the same method. The key point is to record my best thoughts before they get diluted by the comparatively arduous task of preparing a complete presentation.

Once the synopsis is done, then the blindfold can come off and the rest of the creation process is straightforward. Since I now have a plan, it has suddenly become much easier to select from existing slides. I put aside those that, however pretty, would get in the way of my message. Of course, I may not be able to cover everything with available material, but at least I will have a clear idea of the gaps to fill. This is where I can create new material (and that doesn't necessarily mean new slides).

The key to this approach is therefore to write an effective synopsis and, for that, it helps to have a tool. I will therefore explain William Freeman's TWO-MINUTE MESSAGE (TMM— also known as an 'elevator pitch').

109

The TWO-MINUTE MESSAGE (TMM)

Even if I master certain knowledge and skills, so that
I am able to respond to questions clearly and deal
with problems competently, there is still a
substantial effort to make when communicating
that knowledge and those skills to others *in a
presentation format*. This is because
presentation formats are linear—one thing after
another—whereas our brains store information in a
highly parallel, associative way. Hence, no matter how well I
know a subject, the business of transforming it into a presentation
or a document is not trivial.

The TMM is a four-part format that helps me to organise my
thoughts into a (linear) synopsis. This synopsis may then either be
used directly to support a short, oral presentation, or it can be
treated as a plan for the production of a longer presentation or
document. The four parts are:

1. *Audience Context Statement (ACS):* A few sentences that
   attract the intended audience's attention to my topic.

2. *Key Statement (KS):* The main message or concept to be
   presented.

3. *Supporting Statements (SS):* A list of statements that back
   up the Key Statement with data and arguments.

4. *Closing Statement (CS):* One or two sentences that
   complete the story begun by the Audience Context
   Statement, drive home the Key Statement and suggest
   next steps.

The first three statements must be completely non-overlapping.
That is, the Audience Context Statement must not mention
anything that is also covered by the Key Statement. Likewise, the
Key Statement and the Supporting Statements must be distinct.
The Closing Statement, by its very nature, must overlap the other
statements, since its job is to recap the entire TMM in a
memorable way, linking to some future actions.

To reiterate a point made above, my TMM must consist of
complete sentences, *not* bullet points. I should be able to read out

---

A TMM to promote TMMs

Audience Context Statement: Customer-Facing Engineers are generally under time pressure and so the work of preparing presentations has to be done as quickly as possible. They therefore need a way to produce high-impact presentations quickly, reusing old material as necessary, but without falling into the copy-and-paste trap.

Key Statement: By starting preparations with the production of a MAP and a TWO-MINUTE MESSAGE (TMM), rather than by looking at old material, CFEs end up delivering more original and more impactful presentations.

Supporting Statements: Please see the *In Brief* section of this chapter.

Closing Statement: The use of MAP and TMM to prepare presentations and other documents allows CFEs to stand out from the crowd when it matters most: when they need to impress customers and colleagues. While simple and easy to remember, expert use of the procedure requires practice, and so the reader is encouraged to use every writing and presentation opportunity to become more proficient.

---

a TMM as though it were a short story. Taking this approach guarantees that the ideas in the TMM are properly thought out and captured in an unambiguous way so that, later, I remember clearly what I meant when I wrote them. This also helps when collaborating with others on a TMM.

Although the MAP + TMM procedure is straightforward, it is tricky to execute it well. It is the discipline with which it is carried out that determines the quality of the result. To help with this, I will now give a few more details on each of the sections, with some examples.[19]

Audience Context Statement (ACS)

In my experience, many people find it difficult to understand what is meant by 'Audience Context Statement' when they first hear the term. Other authors call this the 'Warmer' or the 'Opening Statement', but I prefer Freeman's original term because the words 'Audience' and 'Context' really say what the statement is all about.

---

[19] Please refer to the web pages associated with this book or to William Freeman, *The Two Minute Message* (Freeman 2000) for further examples.

Taking these two words in reverse order, the Audience Context Statement must capture the *context* of the presentation since, without the necessary background, the message may be misinterpreted or not make sense at all. For example, suppose I were to walk into a meeting room where the people already present had just been discussing urgent bug fixes for a product. Their thinking is likely to be focused on short-term solutions to the product crisis. If my presentation is about the company's long-term product strategy, it will be necessary to define this context before I launch into the details of the multi-year roadmap.

When defining the context, the key is to make its definition audience-focused—hence the 'Audience' part of Audience Context Statement. If, for example, I am about to present a software tool for the first time, an effective statement would refer to the design challenges that the audience can address with the tool (but without mentioning the tool itself!). A weak Audience Context Statement would be, for example, something that describes recent trends in related software technology. The latter might concern me, as a software provider, but is likely to be of less interest to the audience who probably care less about how the software is built than what it can do.

As mentioned above, the Audience Context Statement and the Key Statement must not overlap: hence, when I write the TMM I take care not to refer to anything that is in the main part of the presentation. It's like painting the background of a picture. If the subject of the picture is a house, then not a single brick must appear in the Audience Context Statement.

The last paragraph notwithstanding, the Audience Context Statement sets the audience up for the Key Statement (some authors prefer the term 'Warmer', since the purpose of the Audience Context Statement is to 'warm the audience up' for what follows). In order to do so it must, of course, be sufficiently interesting to capture their attention.

The style of the Audience Context Statement will depend on many factors: the size of the audience, the setting, my personal style, local custom, and so on. One factor is particularly important, however: who initiated the presentation.

When I produce a presentation or document in response to someone's request (i.e. *reactively*), the context is defined by that request. Hence, the Audience Context Statement must start with an acknowledgement, and maybe a playback, of that request. This will reassure the audience that I have understood what they are asking for. If, on the other hand, I am producing a presentation or document *proactively*, then my Audience Context Statement must suggest a context. This will help the audience to understand the relevance of the presentation or document to them.

For example, if I am summoned to a client's offices to make a presentation about issues that they are seeing in our products, then my Audience Context Statement would *not* be about the market challenges that my client is seeing. It would state that there are certain product issues and that, as far as I understand, the client would like a summary of their causes and the measures being taken to put things right. If, on the other hand, I have suggested that a presentation of some of our new technology might be interesting to my client, my Audience Context Statement will describe the business context that justifies this suggestion.

In summary, an Audience Context Statement must (1) be relevant to the audience, (2) catch their attention and (3) provide the background for the Key Statement without mentioning any part of it explicitly. The style of the Audience Context Statement will depend strongly on whether the presentation is being made reactively or proactively.

The Audience Context Statement for this book

'For a technology-based company to realise the potential value of its products and services, its field teams must communicate efficiently and effectively. Achieving this goal in a high-pressure, B2B environment, often with geographically dispersed, cross-cultural teams, is a major challenge.'

This Audience Context Statement is proactive and it is aimed at B2B audiences. It says nothing about the book itself, but it does introduce the context that makes the book relevant.

Key Statement (KS)

The Key Statement is the main message or concept to be presented.

This must be *singular*, and so I pay careful attention to any occurrence of the word 'and' in my Key Statement. Making a choice of one, and only one, Key Statement is important (and often difficult).

As I write this, I can hear the protests of engineers tasked with making product presentations, or even product training courses, where the idea is to have the audience understand many features or functions. How can it be possible to identify a single, main message when there are so many things to present?

A first answer to this is given in the subsection below, 'Order of Implementation for MAP + TMM', where I suggest starting the work of writing a TMM with the Supporting Statements. Once all the Supporting Statements are listed, it may be easier to see a point that stands out as being particularly important, and this would become the Key Statement.

A second answer is to step back from the presentation and to try to identify a statement that transcends the detail of the main part of the presentation. This is linked to my previous suggestion, since listing the Supporting Statements may help in doing this.

⑨ **EXAMPLE** For example, in the case of a presentation for a product that has hundreds of hardware and software features—a camera, say— a Key Statement might be: 'Based on our understanding of your product inspection needs, this camera has all the features that you require for the next 18 months of operations.'

The Key Statement for this book

'This book equips Customer-Facing Engineers with the ICON9® toolkit, allowing them to support sales and deliver solutions in a methodical, authentic manner that strongly favours profitable outcomes.'

This is an example of how to write a Key Statement for a product that contains many features, as mentioned above. Rather than focusing on one feature of the book, I step back and pass a higher-level message.

Another example—the presentation of a new microprocessor architecture to a group of design engineers. In this case, a Key Statement might be: 'This three-hour presentation will give you a broad overview of the main features of the architecture—enough for design planning, but not enough for detailed implementation work.' This is *the* thing that I want the audience to understand, since I wish to avoid giving them the impression that a three-hour talk will make them experts in the architecture.

A final example, where the presentation is in response to a client complaint: 'Our main concern is to reassure you that we will fix this problem in a way that minimises any further impact on your operations.' Note that, in the latter case, the Audience Context Statement would have shown an understanding of the impact that the problem had already had on the client's operations.

Supporting Statements (SS)

As mentioned, the Supporting Statements are usually the easiest statements to write. There is no limit to the number of Supporting Statements. Having listed them, I can simply select the ones that are most important to include in the final presentation or document, according to the time or space available.

The key thing to note about the Supporting Statements is that they must genuinely support the Key Statement—not compete with it. If, after the presentation, I ask a member of the audience to identify the Key Statement, they should be able to do so, without confusion with the Supporting Statements.

The Supporting Statements describing this book correspond to the items listed in the Detailed Table of Contents, in Annex 3.

Closing Statement (CS)

I end with the beginning in mind. That is, the Closing Statement must:

- ❑ Refer to the context that was described in the Audience Context Statement
- ❑ Reinforce the Key Statement one last time in a brief, memorable way
- ❑ Lead the audience towards some concrete next steps with a recommendation or request.

9
EXAMPLE
For a proactive presentation about a new camera, a Closing Statement could be: 'For the production challenges that you have described, the GZ4923 camera would seem to be an excellent choice, given that it is available now and completely covers your needs for the next 18 months. Would you like us to set up a technical evaluation?'

This Closing Statement refers to the context (the production challenges that the client has described), to the Key Statement (that the camera in question covers the needs foreseen for the 18 months to come) and suggests some follow-up actions.

9
EXAMPLE
For a reactive presentation, such as the earlier case of responding to a client complaint, a Closing Statement might look like this: 'Rest assured that we do understand the impact that this problem is having on your production (*link to Audience Context Statement*), and that the actions we are taking will get you back to normal with minimum further disruption (*reiterating the Key Statement*). However, since this is going to take about a week, and you are obviously not going to feel comfortable until it's over, I suggest that we have short status calls every day until we're done (*link to next steps*).'

The Closing Statement for this book

'The ICON9 toolkit addresses the needs of engineers working in challenging commercial environments. By providing a structure for client encounters, it makes successful outcomes more probable, and it supports the continuous improvement of skills and processes. By providing tools for the job, it helps engineers to support clients efficiently while protecting their own interests and those of their organisations. By keeping things simple, it makes these benefits accessible to busy individuals and it allows the methods to be shared across teams. To get a copy of the book …'

This Closing Statement links to the Audience Context Statement (the challenging commercial environment), the Key Statement (links to the toolkit, its audience and its value) and it suggests a next step.

Order of Implementation for MAP + TMM

Although the ACS–KS–SS–CS sequence is the logical one as far as the final presentation is concerned, it is often easier to implement things in a different order. This is because one of the toughest jobs in producing the TMM synopsis is to identify the Key Statement. It must be singular, and selecting just one message is hard to do.

Hence, rather than start with this task, it is sometimes easier to begin by listing the Supporting Statements, from which a Key Statement may emerge. Now, since the Audience Context Statement has to lead to the Key Statement, it is tricky to write it before knowing the Key Statement. The Closing Statement depends on the Audience Context Statement and the Key Statement, and so it makes sense for this to be at the end of the sequence. With all this in mind, it can often make sense to tackle the elements of MAP and TMM in the following order:

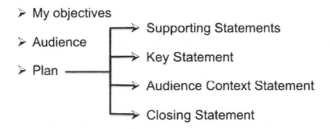

- ➤ My objectives
- ➤ Audience
- ➤ Plan
  - ➤ Supporting Statements
  - ➤ Key Statement
  - ➤ Audience Context Statement
  - ➤ Closing Statement

The Importance of Starting Blindfold

I have emphasised the importance of starting creative activities, such as preparing presentations and documents, 'blindfold'. Recall that this means conceiving my main ideas *before being influenced* by anyone else's. Two examples illustrate why this is so important.

The film *Now You See Me* opens with a card trick (easy to find on YouTube). A magician asks me to watch as he quickly fans a deck of cards, to see if I notice one card in particular. I (the film-watching

audience) see the cards and make a mental note of one of them. The magician then throws the cards in the air and, as the camera sweeps up, I see the windows of a nearby building light up to form the seven of diamonds. Of course, that was the card that I had noticed. I was influenced somehow. I chose a card, but somehow it was not my choice.

My second example comes from the chapter on 'Anchors' in Danielle Kahneman's book *Thinking Fast and Slow* (Kahneman 2013). Visitors to the San Francisco Exploratorium were asked two questions:

> ▸ Is the height of the tallest redwood tree more or less than 1,200 feet?
>
> ▸ What is your best guess at the height of the tallest redwood?

Other visitors were asked the same questions, but with 1,200 feet replaced with 180 feet in the first. As you may have guessed, the two groups produced very different mean estimations for the second question: 844 feet and 282 feet. That is, one estimate is about three times higher than the other!

Both the above examples demonstrate how impressionable we are. Our subconscious is easily influenced.

If I start a creative piece of work by looking at existing PowerPoint presentations, doing internet searches, looking at books and asking others, the result is unlikely to contain my spark of originality. It may be 'OK', but will the key message or concept be my own, or will it be a rehash of ideas that I've just seen (hence boring the audience, who have also seen these ideas before)?

Of course, it's important to refer to the existing material at some point. However, by doing this *after* I've done some original thinking, I both increase my chances of producing an interesting result and make my search for existing material more effective. Having written a TMM, I will be more acutely aware of what I'm looking for and this will help me both to find it (e.g. using the right keywords) and to recognise it (e.g. the slide that does the job, not necessarily the most visually impressive one).

Presenting Empty-Handed

Although the TMM was conceived as an intermediate step to creating another document, such as a presentation, it may also be an end in itself. I have found that a TMM and, above all, the effort that goes into creating it, is a first-rate support for an 'empty-handed' presentation. That is, a presentation for which I have no pre-prepared slides or other support.

I discovered the use of the TMM to support empty-handed presentations when running a CFE training course. While working on the preparation of presentations with the trainees, I had the idea of asking a participant to abandon the slides that he had just created and do his presentation using the whiteboard only. Not only was the presentation extremely good—clear, entertaining and on-subject—the presenter enjoyed himself tremendously!

There were a couple of reasons for this:

▸ Without the barrier of having slides to present, the presenter was better able to make contact with the audience. This was more fun for him and them.

▸ Having worked hard on his TMM, the presenter had a clear idea of how he intended to attract the audience's attention, what message he wished to pass on, and so on. Not only was he able to present this: he was in an excellent position to respond to questions and adapt to the audience's needs. He had assimilated the TMM completely and was therefore confident and comfortable.

While I do not recommend abandoning PowerPoint, I have had many occasions since the one described above to notice how TMM-based preparation strengthens the presenter's hand. It is crucial to be able to present without slides, even if it's not necessary to do so.

Different Ways to Use the TMM

A TMM is usually an initial step in a process to prepare a presentation or a document. The good news is that, once I have written my TMM, I am free to do whatever I want. The bad news —you guessed it—is also that I am free to do whatever I want …

Creative freedom has a price: choices have to be made and this takes time. Since time is at a premium, I will now give some examples of next steps for:

▸ Short presentations (say, 5–10 minutes)

▸ Challenger presentations (for surprising, new ideas)

▸ Lengthy presentations

▸ Other types of document.

From a TMM to a Short Presentation

A simple mapping from a TMM to a short, slide-based presentation is shown in the diagram below:

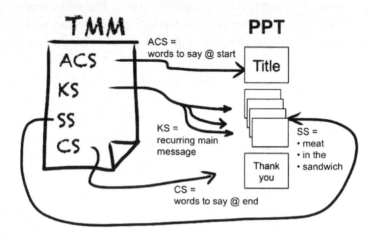

For a presentation of say, 5 to 10 minutes in length, it is key to get and retain my audience's attention for the entire length of the talk.

The worst way to begin would therefore be to show a complicated slide and to explain its contents. Worse still would be to look at the slides as I read them. My audience would immediately think 'Here we go again', and switch off. The conscientious ones might start reading the slides, but they wouldn't be paying much attention to me.

For this reason, I like to deal with the Audience Context Statement part of the TMM, which is there to set the scene and grab the audience's attention, without slides. The title slide of the talk may be shown, but this contains only two or three words and is not a distraction. I establish eye contact with the audience and say something like: 'Good morning. I'm happy to have this opportunity to talk to you about ... today. As you may know ... (*Audience Context Statement*).'

If the Audience Context Statement requires slide support then, of course, I will use some, but only after I have started with some engaging words to the background of a title slide.

For a short presentation, I may not need to show the agenda and objectives on slides. Even if they are not shown explicitly, however, I quickly explain the structure of my talk after the Audience Context Statement.

I would be justified in using PAGE for this:[20] the Purpose corresponds to the Audience Context Statement. The Agenda and Goals follow, then, before diving into the detail of the talk, I get an Endorsement from my audience. The latter may vary from a few grunts in the case of a large audience (in a conference situation, for example) to a meaningful exchange if I am presenting to a handful of clients. Such an exchange can even lead me to revise my presentation plan (by dropping some topics and emphasising others, for example).

Next comes the Key Statement. This generally requires a slide, and a slide all to itself! Recall that the key statement must be singular, and a strong point of focus.

---

[20] See Chapter 4.

The Supporting Statements follow the Key Statement, and this is where any on-the-fly adaptations to my talk may come in. Depending on the nature of the audience and their response to my post-ACS questions (see above), I may decide to emphasise certain Supporting Statements at the expense of others. However this goes, I refer back to my Key Statement during the presentation of the support whenever it makes sense.

To finish the talk, I like to make the Closing Statement in the same way that I made the Audience Context Statement: I abandon my slides once again and turn to the audience. As I deliver my Closing Statement, there are no slides or any other distractions. In this way I ensure that I have everyone's attention and increase my chances of some productive discussion.

From a TMM to a Challenger Presentation

The Corporate Executive Board (CEB), a market research organisation, has published a sales methodology called 'Challenger' (DixonAdamson 2011). A strong theme in the Challenger methodology is that, for complex sales, it is often necessary to present the client with an alternative way of viewing a situation, to help them see needs that they were previously unaware of (this is a highly simplified summary, of course). To enable Salespeople to do this, the CEB describes a method for delivering a 'Reframe' presentation.

A Reframe presentation starts with a 'Warmer', which is essentially an Audience Context Statement. It sets the scene.

What follows is the Reframe itself, which is a short, surprising message, liable to give the client a jolt. For example, 'In 20 years' time, digital cameras will dominate your industry' would have been a good Reframe message to have given to Kodak in 1980. In TMM terms, this is the Key Statement.

Of course, the Reframe needs support, just as any Key Statement does, and the CEB suggests it be structured as follows:

1. Facts, figures, statistics
2. How this affects the client
3. New possibilities
4. A solution.

The CEB has its own terminology for these four points, but we might recognise them as the steps of the SUBROUTINE: Situation–Problems–Needs–Solutions. This is, in fact, an extremely good way to structure the Supporting Statements. First, elaborate the Situation in more detail (e.g a summary of early digital camera technology and statistics on their dramatic development potential). Then demonstrate how this Situation may affect the client (digital cameras don't need film—this is a Problem). Based on this, what Needs are now apparent (Kodak has to embrace the new technology, exploit its status as an inventor, explore new ways of exploiting its dominant industry position, etc.) and what actions (Solutions) might be envisaged? The Closing Statement then wraps up.

This example remains very close to the TMM in structure, with just the addition of the SUBROUTINE process to organise the Supporting Statements part.

From a TMM to a Lengthy Presentation

In the case of presentations lasting 15 minutes or more, the structure is likely to be completely decoupled from the TMM. It will be determined by factors such as the venue, the presentation length, the size of the audience, and the subject matter itself.

The two checklists below suggest optional elements for inclusion in lengthy presentations and some logistical considerations that might apply on 'significant' occasions.

It can be seen that there are many parameters, and therefore a huge number of permutations of presentation structure. Having a TMM in hand will certainly help me to complete the presentation, since it has captured my ideas in a synthetic form. This allows me to design my presentation structure according to the logistical and other constraints just reviewed, then to map my ideas onto them. The structure of the TMM itself may not be visible in the final presentation, however.

Checklist for Extended Presentations

Potential Beginning Elements	
Title	
Purpose/Objectives	With the agenda, this is essentially the PAGE of the presentation.
Content/Agenda	For long presentations, the agenda can start off each new section.
Organisation/About us (company, group …)	
Executive summary	
Situation statement/Present understanding/Motivation for the subject	
Attention grabber	This could be an amazing slide, or something else, like a demonstration.
Potential Middle Elements	
Subject itself (a product, approach, solution, proposal …)	
Positioning	With respect to the audience, a market or other solutions.
Examples	
Benefits	Explains how a solution will benefit its target audience.
Costs, Risks, Compliance issues …	
Alternative approaches/solutions	
Potential End Elements	
Questions and Answers	Can be in the form of Frequently Asked Questions (FAQ), with pre-prepared answers, or an open forum.
Summary and conclusion	
Thank you	

Checklist of Presentation Logistics

☐ Should I include deliberate pauses, for questions and debate?

☐ Should my presentation include a progress indicator (e.g. a section tag on each slide, or page # of N)?

☐ Is a storyline or running example appropriate, to maintain a thread through the whole presentation?

☐ Should I include confidentiality and/or copyright notices (any need for a Non-Disclosure Agreement?)

☐ What prerequisite knowledge does the audience require?

☐ Are there language and/or cultural barriers?

☐ Are there any staging requirements, such as access to the internet, to power or to machinery?

From a TMM to Other Documents

In some cases, a TMM is almost an end in itself. For example, writing a good 500-word blog comes down to writing a TMM!

It should be no surprise that I used a TMM to plan this book, and I had to rewrite it several times as the work progressed. I also use TMMs when creating documents, articles, presentations and training material on behalf of clients. In these cases, I generally write and ask my client to review the TMM before I get down to writing the full document. In the case of press articles, the TMM forms a part of my commercial quotation. Hence, it is at the heart of my business!

While this section has focused on the TMM, I stress that the process being followed is MAP, and that the TMM constitutes the Plan part. Hence, if you have an alternative method for producing a short synopsis of a document or presentation, by all means use it! The key is to do this 'blindfold'—before looking at the mountain of material that already exists.

In Brief

✦ An excessive dependence on slides to drive client interactions is dangerous.

✦ Start the plan 'blindfold', doing initial preparation without looking at existing material.

✦ For presentations, this initial preparation should start with MAP, and the Plan part of MAP should be a synopsis of the presentation.

✦ The TWO-MINUTE MESSAGE (TMM) synopsis consists of four parts:

• Audience Context Statement

• Key Statement (must be singular)

• Supporting Statements

• Closing Statement.

✦ There are many different ways to go from a completed TMM to a finished presentation or document.

✦ Producing a TMM puts me in a position to make better presentations, and to be able to respond to questions with more assurance, since it helps me to clarify my message to myself.

✦ Steve Jobs did not prepare his presentations by sifting through a mountain of old slides, and neither should we.

TWO-MINUTE MESSAGE

Audience Context, Key, Supporting and Closing Statements

Use in Prepare for Presentations in the Do phase.

Follow Up

Check

Do

Engage

Prepare

8. Challenging and Negotiating: TABLE

'If you think you're too small to have an impact, try going to bed with a mosquito in the room',
Anita Roddick

Excellent work will make an impact, but experience shows that if I constantly strive to meet ever more demanding requirements, then those requirements will become more demanding still. Standing up for myself and my organisation, to firmly and politely resist unreasonable pressure, is one reason to take a challenging stance with respect to clients. A second is for their own good.

Sometimes, my client will have problems or be missing opportunities because they are unable to see all the alternatives available to them. Someone who, a few years ago, was not keeping up with the progress of the internet, for example, would not have been aware of the possibilities for remote technical support that it offered. They would have been stuck with the old 'telephone and on-site visits' model of operating. In such circumstances, a Customer-Facing Engineer could challenge the client's view of the world in order to open up new, network-based support alternatives to them.

Both of these cases—resisting pressure and proposing alternative viewpoints—represent opportunities for a Customer-Facing Engineer to add significant value to their own organisation and to their client's. The people that make the most impact sometimes have to be disobedient—saying 'No', pushing back against requests, walking away from unattractive proposals—and they sometimes make unexpected suggestions. By doing this, they (1) protect themselves, their organisations and (ultimately) their clients from the consequences of unhealthy agreements, and (2) they unlock possibilities that others have not seen.

Tools for Challengers

Two of the tools already discussed in this book are of direct help to CFEs when challenging: the SUBROUTINE and the TMM.

Process 3 of the SUBROUTINE is especially relevant when disagreeing with a client or resisting them in some way. As explained in Chapter 6, I first clarify the Situation as I see it (sticking to the facts and avoiding filtering), then I explain what Problems this Situation is causing me, and what my associated Needs are. The Needs are described at a level which is easy for my client to relate to, since they have similar Needs themselves: to do work of a certain quality, to satisfy the requirements of my parent organisation, to have sufficient time and energy left for my family at the end of the day, and so on. Finally, at the Solutions level, I request that the client take some action or I suggest a next step that we can both contribute to.

This four-step communication process helps me to confront my client without descending into conflict with them. If my client is asking me for something that I consider unreasonable, then an unstructured response could lead me to betray irritation. Since my client no doubt considers that their request *is* reasonable, such a response would risk a clash. To avoid this, the SUBROUTINE leads me to start with verifiable facts, then to describe feelings and Needs which, since they concern only me, nobody can contradict. This approach reduces the chances of my suggestions causing offence and makes it more likely that we will be able to negotiate a Solution acceptable to both parties.

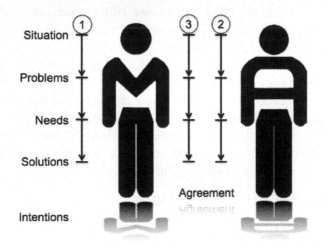

128

The diagram opposite also appeared in Chapter 6, but now has some additions. An Agreement is shown after the final step of the SUBROUTINE process, to represent the result that I hope to achieve when challenging or negotiating with a client. Also, the Agreement and both of the people involved now have reflections, representing aspects of the conversation that cannot readily be seen. I will discuss the unspoken aspect of Agreements in a later section of this chapter, and this is what is represented by the mirror-image of 'Agreement' in the diagram. The reflections of both parties to the conversation are also shown in the diagram, reminding me of an aspect of our psychological states that has an important influence on negotiations: our Intentions. This is also discussed later in the chapter.

The TWO-MINUTE MESSAGE (TMM) can be used to make a challenge in the form of a 'Reframe' presentation (DixonAdamson 2011), as discussed briefly in Chapter 7.

Challenging a support request

Suppose that my client requests that I work on their site for five days straight in order to help them prepare a product release. I use the SUBROUTINE in 'Output Routine' mode (variant #3) in order to politely resist their request, as follows:

'Aude, I understand that your product release deadline is on February 15th and that your team will need help from us to meet this date. At the same time, I have commitments to other clients that I must honour, as do my colleagues (*Situation*). I am anxious to help, though worried that we may not be able to meet your current expectations (*Problem*). It would help me to understand in more detail what assistance you are expecting (*Need*): could you spare half an hour to go through this with me now, so that I can then suggest some alternatives? (*Solution/Request for action*)'

Having made this challenge, I then negotiate a less onerous support commitment while, of course, doing everything I can to facilitate my client's product release.

Challenging a technical specification

My client is frustrated by the power consumption of a video controller that I have supplied, since it is above the power budget for the corresponding part of their design. I reassure them that my device can meet their needs, and suggest a short presentation of its novel features.

The presentation that I give challenges my client's current view on how the functions in their system are distributed amongst its component parts. The TMM for this 'Reframe' presentation is:

Audience Context Statement: We understand that the power budgets for the systems that you are designing are becoming much tighter, as are the profit margins for your finished products.

Key Statement: Our latest video controllers will reduce system power consumption significantly, provided that the overall system architecture is adjusted for their innovative features.

Supporting Statements: (See Chapter 7, *From TMM to Challenger Presentations,* for guidance on this part.)

Closing Statement: The functions of multiple, formally independent devices are now contained in our video controllers. For you to benefit from the power and cost savings that this can give, I suggest that we schedule a working session to go over possible new design scenarios.'

Having made this challenge, I then have to negotiate with my client to change the architecture of their system, reallocating functionality and power budgets and thus displacing other devices (which are perhaps supplied by my competitors).

Recall that a Reframe presentation aims to surprise a client by suggesting an alternative way of viewing a situation. For example, I attended a conference recently where a member of the Highways Agency—an organisation responsible for managing roads in the UK—described the systems for managing traffic flow on crowded motorways. His introduction (Audience Context Statement) easily engaged the audience, since he evoked the traffic problems that most people had endured on their way to the venue. The constant headache of deploying and maintaining motorway equipment was also mentioned.

He then said, 'What if we were to put a lot of this equipment in the cars themselves?' (Key Statement and Reframe) and went on to explain how this could be done (Supporting Statements).

This is an example of where a well-structured presentation can surprise an audience and lead them to change their viewpoint. It opens up new possibilities and needs (I realise that I will need a car that understands dynamic speed limits, for example), and leads me to consider new solutions (e.g. to drive a modern car, rather than the wrecks that I normally run around in).

Both the SUBROUTINE and the TMM can be used to make a challenge, but this is not the end of the story. Having been challenged, a client needs to understand what to do next. If they make a request that I refuse, then what? If I show them a different way of looking at their situation, how do they take advantage of this new perspective? Since I am confronting them, either with resistance or new ideas, I must then lead them to alternative solutions and negotiate their implementation.

From Challenging to Negotiating

When asked, CFEs typically state that they do little negotiation in their jobs, and that it is the role of Salespeople and executives to look after commercial and financial matters. However, negotiation does not have to involve money. Time, resources and know-how are all negotiable items. Whether I am discussing a meeting agenda, the details of a software licence or the amount of beer to order for the end-of-year party, negotiation skills are needed.

Further, a CFE's work underpins negotiations that are made by their Salespeople and executives, and being in tune with them on negotiation strategy and techniques is crucial for effective teamwork. I know several engineers who have played a key part in company acquisitions, for example. They have been involved on account of their technical expertise, of course, but it is impossible to contribute at this level without good business acumen and negotiation skills.

Negotiation is an ever-present aspect of an encounter. I therefore need to raise my awareness of its presence and pay attention to the rules and guidelines that govern negotiation.

The good news is that all of the tools and methods that have been discussed so far in this book are applicable to negotiations. From the Encounter Process, through MAP, PAGE and the TMM to the SUBROUTINE, all of these fundamental techniques constitute a foundation for effective communication, which is a prerequisite to successful negotiation. In addition, a mastery of certain negotiation-specific concepts, such as those captured in the following tool, is of great value to CFEs.

The TABLE

The TABLE brings MAP together with the following negotiation concepts:

▸ Exchanges

▸ Fall Lines

▸ Fallbacks

▸ Fallout.

The TABLE captures critical pre-negotiation thoughts and, in doing so, frees up my mind for the potentially difficult job of challenging my client. It helps me to define my bargaining position and to decide what to do if an agreement is not reached: things that require careful consideration, and that I would not want to improvise during the discussion itself.

The tool, shown on the next page, uses MAP as a front end, since it is necessary to clarify my objectives and anticipate my audience before starting to negotiate. The Plan part of MAP is used to capture the four negotiation concepts mentioned above.

My Objectives and Audience

These two items were discussed in detail in Chapter 3. In the case of a negotiation, 'My objectives' must include my negotiation targets, of course. Discovery targets are also of prime importance since, as will be discussed, my negotiation approach will be to look for a Solution that satisfies the interests of all parties. To do this, I must first discover these interests.

In the context of a team effort, 'My objectives' (shared by the team) can include restrictions, such as information to protect. Making this explicit in objectives planning can prevent misunderstandings between team members, where one person unwittingly reveals information that another considers to be of tactical importance.

The TABLE										
My objectives	Negotiation target, discovery targets, information to protect ...									
Audience	Anticipating the client negotiator(s), their concerns, etc.									
	Offer?		**Cost to me**				**Value to them**			
	1		1	2	3	4	1	2	3	4
	2		1	2	3	4	1	2	3	4
	3		1	2	3	4	1	2	3	4
	4		1	2	3	4	1	2	3	4
	Request!		**Value to me**				**Cost to them**			
	1		1	2	3	4	1	2	3	4
	2		1	2	3	4	1	2	3	4
Plan	3		1	2	3	4	1	2	3	4
	4		1	2	3	4	1	2	3	4
	Fall Lines (conditions that trigger a pause/rethink)									
	My Fallback (plan B—the best alternative to an agreement)									
	Their Fallback (my assessment of their plan B ...)									
	My Fallout (consequences of no agreement + use of Fallback)									
	Their Fallout (my guess at the consequences for them ...)									

I have no particular comments to make about anticipating the audience beyond those already made in Chapter 3.

Exchanges—Offers and Requests

During a negotiation, I may concede certain resources (hardware, software, engineering time, etc.). Each concession will cost me something, and it will have a certain value for my client. For example, it may cost me very little to send my client a code snippet, but the value to them could be enormous if it allows them to meet a project deadline.

Conversely, the client controls certain resources (money, access to key people, market information, etc.), and they may concede some of them. Such concessions will have a value to me and represent a cost to them.

The global result of a negotiation for each party is the sum of the value of concessions received less the cost of those conceded. This is called the gain—the difference between value obtained and costs incurred. For example, if I pay €20 for a book that is worth €30 to me (i.e. its value to me is €30), then my gain is €10. If the book was only worth €4 to the person selling it and their shipping cost is €6, then their gain is €20-€4-€6 = €10 also.

In this simple case of 'single-issue' negotiation, price is the only parameter. It was chosen because it's easy to quantify. For B2B, we are more concerned with 'multi-issue' negotiation where the cost and value of many parameters are difficult to assess.

Understanding the overall cost–value–gain situation of the parties to a negotiation is key to obtaining a favourable outcome. To achieve this, a summary of potential exchanges, with an idea of their cost and value to each side, is included in the TABLE.[21] It can be seen that concessions that I am ready to offer, in the 'Offer?' section, and concessions that I wish to receive in return, in the 'Request!' section, are listed with their associated costs and values. Since it is generally impractical to put a monetary value on these items, a scale of 1–4 is used.

For example, an agreement about a product evaluation may involve coming to terms on the length of the evaluation, the

---

[21] This is also called a 'concessions table' or a 'trade-offs table' in the literature.

Offer?		Cost to me				Value to them			
1	6 week evaluation instead of 4	1	**2**	3	4	1	2	**3**	4
2	4 software licences (instead of 2)	**1**	2	3	4	1	2	**3**	4
3	direct consulting help	1	2	3	**4**	1	2	3	**4**
4	free training	1	2	**3**	4	1	2	**3**	4
Request!		**Value to me**				**Cost to them**			
1	agreement to purchase if all ok	1	2	3	**4**	1	2	3	**4**
2	access to their top management	1	2	3	**4**	1	**2**	3	4
3	remote access to their system	1	2	**3**	4	1	**2**	3	4
4		1	2	3	4	1	2	3	4

product features concerned, the number of people involved on each side, the location of the work, the licensing and hosting of any software involved, and so on. The figure above shows how this might look in the 'Exchanges' part of the TABLE.

It can be seen that conceding two extra software licences to my client represents a very low cost to me, but has a quite high value to them (line 2 of the 'Offer?' section). This is therefore a concession that I am quite prepared to make. However, in order to achieve a balanced outcome, I should take care to request corresponding concessions. The concession that has the highest value to me, while representing a reasonable cost to my client (as far as I can tell), is for access to their top management (line 2 of the 'Request!' section).

Completing this part of the TABLE prior to a negotiation meeting has two major benefits for me and my colleagues. Firstly, it clarifies the anticipated situation, freeing up the minds of the negotiators for the negotiation conversation itself. Without this preparation it would be necessary to consider the trade-offs represented in the table while in front of the client, and I could easily make a mistake. This kind of work is best done offline.

The second benefit is for teams. Possible exchanges can be considered collaboratively, thus ensuring that all the stakeholders for a negotiation (whether they will be present in the client discussions or not) can give their inputs on the trade-offs to make. This can be important when, for example, a Sales and Applications team is negotiating the specification of a bespoke or customised product with a client. Once the specification is agreed, it will be handed over to a Product Development team for implementation. The Product Developers are therefore important stakeholders, even if they will not be present at the negotiations.

Fall Lines

Fall Lines delimit a 'search space' of negotiation Solutions within which I am comfortable. I don't like the look of the Solutions outside of this space, beyond the Fall Lines, and so when the negotiation approaches one, then alarms go off in my head. They may cause me to break off negotiations temporarily in order to rethink my position and perhaps consult with others.

The term 'Fall Line' is a geographical one. It defines the limit of a plateau of hard rock. Beyond the limit, the softer rock is eroded away by the action of rivers and streams, so that the latter drop at the Fall Line, forming rapids and waterfalls. If I imagine the plateau as being a Solution space, where each position on it represents a different compromise between the various negotiation parameters, then the Fall Line represents the acceptable limit of that space as far as I am concerned.

Fall Lines (conditions that trigger a pause/consultation/rethink)

No agreement by the 20th: call boss (he is concerned to close by month end)

If they neither agree to give us access to their top management, nor make a commitment to purchase the product if the evaluation is OK: pause!

This example, for a negotiation concerning a product evaluation, reuses the scenario introduced for the Exchanges part of the TABLE, above.

Continuing the example from above, if my client stubbornly refuses to attach any commitment to a successful completion of the product evaluation, then I may feel that this refusal is taking me too close to my Fall Line. At the moment, I cannot envisage a negotiation solution that does not include this commitment. In response to my alarms going off I may say, 'I understand that it is difficult for you to make that commitment, but it leaves me in a tricky position. Without it, I can't commit the resources needed to ensure the evaluation's success. Let me go away and talk to my boss about this, and I'll get back to you.'

A Fall Line is not the same as the well-known concept of a Bottom Line, which is a hard limit set on one negotiation parameter. Bottom Lines are much less flexible than Fall Lines, since they introduce rigidity into the negotiation process, reducing the size of the solution 'search space'.

A second reason for avoiding Bottom Lines is that they tend to act as anchors, pulling the negotiation in their direction. For example, if a Bottom Line is financial, such as the lowest price at which I am prepared to sell something, then my client will be very keen to find out what that price is. Once they find out, it will be very hard to raise the price above that line!

In practice, a Bottom Line is often set by a manager who is delegating some kind of negotiation task to a collaborator: 'Mike, please call Aude and fix a date for the review meeting. No later than the end of the month!' Hence, the Bottom Line is the end of the month, and it is a constraint imposed by the manager. In these circumstances, a sensible option is to treat the constraint not as a

> **Bottom Line on the number of trainees (deprecated)**
> It might be tempting to set a Bottom Line when negotiating the number of people that a client can send to a training course: a non-negotiable maximum of 16 participants, say. I see two major problems with this approach:
>   Let's say that my choice of Bottom Line is motivated by the fact that the training course will be in a foreign country. I'm worried that the language barrier will make it hard to handle more than 16 trainees. There are other solutions to this problem. For example, one or two of the trainees with good language skills might act as facilitators, thus making it easy for me to handle more people. This Solution could be good for both me and my client ... and we would miss it if I introduced and stuck to a Bottom Line.

Bottom Line, but as one of my Fall Lines. Hence, if it turns out to be difficult to agree a date for the review meeting before the end of the month, then I refer back to my manager.

Note that I can have multiple Fall Lines, and that they can be described quantitatively or qualitatively. This reflects the complex, multi-issue nature of most B2B negotiations.[22]

Fallback and Fallout

Two more 'Fall' parameters are also crucial to pre-negotiation planning: my Fallback and the Fallout. What will I do if the negotiation fails? What are the consequences of not getting an agreement?

For example, if my client will not commit to making some kind of purchase should their evaluation of our product be successful, what will we do? Support their evaluation anyway, at a reduced level of effort? Politely disengage? Or something else?

The Fallback is the best alternative that I can see,[23] and understanding my Fallback considerably strengthens my

---

[22] In contrast, a single-issue negotiation has only one parameter, such as price. Market stall negotiations are typically single-issue, where the merchandise is a fixed commodity such as a hat, a pot or a chicken.

[23] In Fisher & Ury's *Getting to Yes* (Fisher, UryPatton 1991), the Fallback is called the BATNA—Best Alternative To a Negotiated Agreement.

My Fallback (plan B—the best alternative to an agreement)

Suggest that we come back to them again in six month's time (after our next product update, say).

Use time that would have been spent on the evaluation to build a product demonstration, for use with other prospects.

This example continues with the case of the evaluation, as do the text boxes that follow.

---

negotiating position. Put another way, not having a Fallback is a massive handicap in negotiation, since it puts the other person in a position of power over me. If I can't afford to walk away, then I am obliged to accept my client's ultimatum. I am weakened because I can't countenance a non-agreement.

The Fallout is a related concept. If we don't achieve an agreement, then clearly there will be some consequences. These can be both positive and negative, as demonstrated by the example in the text box above.

My Fallout (consequences of no agreement + use of Fallback)

Steve *(my Sales colleague)* is going to be unhappy as his pipeline is nearly empty.

Not supporting this evaluation would free up time and resources.

The Fallback and Fallout apply equally well to both parties in the negotiation, of course. My client will have a Fallback, and there will be Fallout for them if no deal is made. Working out my client's Fallback and Fallout can be a key to negotiating a favourable agreement since, if I know their alternatives to a negotiated agreement, then I can more easily estimate the strength of any proposal that I make.

It can also make sense to discuss Fallbacks and Fallout with my client, since they may have a false impression of mine or perhaps an optimistic idea of their own. The latter situation is

139

Their Fallback (my assessment of their plan B …)

Continue to use products from Trivollis *(our competition)*. Push Trivollis for product improvements based on what they have learned from us :-(

!! Rumour is that Trivollis are not going to stay in this business …

---

common. For example, a client might think that their Fallback is to take a solution from my competition, and that this is a good alternative for them. Knowing my competition well, and understanding the weaknesses in their offering, I can see that my client's Fallback is not as strong as they imagine. It is in both of our interests that the real situation is revealed, and so I have to educate my client on their own Fallback and Fallout positions.

Their Fallout (my assessment of the consequences for them …)

Without our product, theirs will become obsolete within a year.

They won't have to put resource into the evaluation (+ve for them).

Negotiation in a B2B Context

The remainder of this chapter discusses further encounter topics that are particularly important when challenging and negotiating.

Collaborative Problem Solving

In the B2B context, interests-based negotiation techniques which aim for a Win–Win outcome are almost always to be favoured. That is, the needs/interests of both parties must be met sufficiently well for them to feel satisfied with the negotiation result. If not, the long-term relationship between the parties will suffer. This implies finding a balance of multiple parameters, such as those mentioned in the evaluation example, above, and illustrated below.

The negotiation process has many of the characteristics of a collaboration, in the sense that the parties work together to find a Solution to this multi-parameter, multi-constraint problem. There is more to it than this, however, since each Solution represents a different gain or loss for each party. For this reason, people who are good at collaborative Solution finding are not always good negotiators.

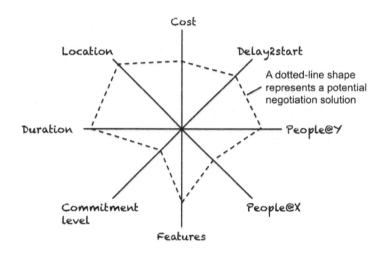

In my experience, CFEs are generally at ease with finding collaborative Solutions, but they can be naive negotiators, caring more about whether a Solution is 'right' than whether it is favourable. Perhaps this is because they place a high value on correct scientific method? Whatever the answer, the TABLE can help, since it highlights the interests-balancing problem. In doing so, it allows the search for a technically correct Solution to be tempered and influenced by the interests of the parties.

It follows that achieving a balanced agreement requires an ability to defend one's interests. In some situations, differences in the negotiation strengths—the power—of each party make this particularly difficult.

Power Differences

If, in spite of my best efforts at persuasion, a powerful negotiating adversary does not accept my proposals, then there is little I can do about it. This is why the life of CFEs working for small suppliers can be frustrating when the client is, say, Apple, Bosch or Samsung.

More serious than this frustration, however, is the danger that I will agree to do something that is against my interests because of pressure from a powerful client. Faced with such pressure, all I can do is limit my losses.

The first need in this situation is to stay 'centred' or 'grounded'. This means that I must remain unperturbed by the pressure and in contact with my own feelings and interests (see page 84 and the use of the SUBROUTINE for achieving a sense of clarity and control).

Remaining centred makes it possible to exert self-control, and to make appropriate use of my Fallback. When my negotiating power is very much smaller than that of my client, having a Fallback option and the ability to use it are my best allies.

Staying in control

A powerful client suddenly announces that they will cease doing business with my company at the end of the year if I don't agree to their support demands. I feel a surge of unpleasant emotions. However, my self-awareness and self-control are good, so I recognise these emotions *without being submerged by them*. My ability to reason therefore remains intact and I am able to make a considered, professional response.

Working with Constraints

In searching for a balanced, Win–Win solution to a negotiation challenge, I must take into account certain constraints on the parameters involved, both external and self-imposed.

External constraints often come from my own organisation and they include time constraints, other forms of Bottom Line, and limits on my authority (for example, I may have to refer to others before making certain concessions to my client). The logical way to manage such constraints is, before the main negotiation, to negotiate with my organisation (Delivré 2013). Note that all of the constraints just mentioned have their uses. Negotiating on behalf of an organisation that didn't impose any would be very difficult: a bit like trying to order a meal for someone who won't say what they prefer to eat. I could order something that I think is delicious, only to find out that it isn't to their taste.

Self-imposed constraints include:[24]

▶ An inner drive to please others

▶ An inner drive to be perfect (never to fail)

▶ An inner drive to be strong

▶ An inner drive to work hard

▶ An inner drive to do everything as quickly as possible.

These five drivers are personality traits, and they can have a strong influence on the way that I behave during a negotiation—especially if I have traits that I'm not aware of.

Know thyself

Someone with a tendency to try to please others may find it hard to take a firm line if their client starts to show signs of unhappiness.

People with a strong drive never to fail may find it hard to walk away without an agreement, thus leaving them vulnerable to accepting deals that are against their interests.

Someone with a need to be strong may find it hard to make certain concessions, even if they are appropriate.

A hard worker may end up not seeing the wood for the trees—getting so bogged down in the detail of a negotiation that they miss an important, strategic point.

Someone who tries to do everything as quickly as possible may tend to skip encounter steps and pay the price for doing so.

As for the earlier discussion on becoming 'centred' or 'grounded', the key to managing these drivers is, firstly, self-awareness, then self-control.

---

[24] These self-imposed constraints correspond to the 'drivers' concept in Transactional Analysis (StewartJoines 1987).

Understanding Agreements and Contracts

All contracts are agreements, but not all agreements are contracts, the difference being that a contract (whether it be written or not) requires commitments from the involved parties, whereas an agreement does not have to.

Eric Berne, the father of Transactional Analysis,[25] defined a contract as 'an explicit bilateral commitment to a well-defined course of action'. He also pointed out that agreements and contracts are either explicit or secret (psychological—Delivré 2013). That is, some things that are not spoken out loud can still form a contract between the parties (see the text box opposite).

A further complication arises when more than two parties are involved in a negotiation. In fact, as far as CFEs are concerned, this situation is the norm, since my client and I represent our

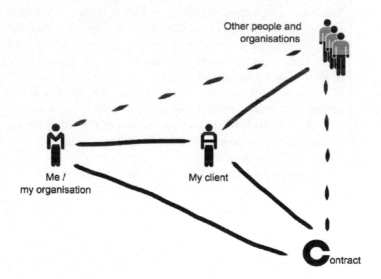

organisations.[26] The negotiation situation is represented in the diagram above. For simplicity, the picture assumes that I am in sync with interested parties within my organisation, and so they

---

[25] See Berne 1964, StewartJoines 1987, Delivré 2004 and Delivré 2013.

[26] François Delivré explains the different personal and professional personas relevant to negotiation (Delivré 2013).

A psychological (secret) contract

Suppose that I am negotiating with my client who is having problems with some circuit boards that have one of my chips integrated in them. The issues certainly involve this chip, but it is not certain that it is really the source of the problems. They are asking for my help to understand what is amiss. Specifically, they want my company to use its diagnostics laboratory to help them.

After some negotiation we might agree that my company will help on a 'best efforts' basis, providing that their company supplies at least six boards that show the problems and that one of their test engineers is available to assist with the debug. That would be the explicit contract.

A secret (psychological) contract between me and my client could be that they will defend me and my company when the going gets tough and their top managers are looking for someone to blame for their production delays. This understanding, even though it is not spoken, has real significance.

The fact that this part of the contract is not made explicit does not mean that it is clandestine (though it can be). Secret contracts are used appropriately when it would be too laborious, or even counterproductive, to elaborate an aspect of an agreement.

---

are not shown explicitly. The solid lines represent the official relationships affecting the negotiation, and the dotted lines show other relationships that may also be important. To manage such situations, it is important that I pay as much attention to the *relationships* as to the *content* of the contract itself. While my negotiation objective may be to achieve particular terms (i.e. content), a contract that cannot be implemented has no value. Hence, if there are stakeholders in my client's organisation that will influence either the content or the implementation of the contract, then I must take them into account.

Salespeople are well aware of this type of dependency. In their case, the contract is a purchase agreement and usually they negotiate with people who don't have the final say on whether an order is placed. The client depends on their managers, on legal and financial services and maybe on other stakeholders.

Similarly, if I am negotiating the installation of some software with a design manager I may discover that another manager, the head of the internal computer service, is in the critical path. There is no point in coming to an agreement with the design manager that will be blocked by the computer service manager, and so I must ensure that this person is aligned. I can do this by talking to them directly, or by motivating my client to do so.

With the above in mind, I suggest that contracts should obey the 'M and M rule'.[27] That is, they must be:

CHECKLIST

☐ Manageable

- Terms are clear enough so that any reasonable person could determine if they are met or not. Where possible, therefore, they are numerical and measurable.

- The resources involved are under the control (direct or indirect) of the main stakeholders. In this respect, an important resource is time.

☐ Motivational

- The stakeholders have sufficient interest in the deal to carry out their part of it.

- Whether written or oral, terms are phrased in positive language wherever possible. For example, 'up to one week' rather than 'no more than one week', or 'has the right to six evaluation licences' rather than 'cannot use more than six evaluation licences', and so on.

---

[27] A curiosity: if the M and M of Manageable and Motivational is turned upside down it becomes the W and W of Win–Win. Hence contracts should be MMWW.

Manipulation

The Elephant in the Room

Using the tools and methods seen so far puts me in a good position to handle many negotiation situations. But I have not yet mentioned the elephant in the room: what do I do when confronted with a negotiator who doesn't want to play fair? Surely, if I always use an interests-based approach and aim at Win–Win outcomes, then I will be easy prey for

anyone with a Win–Lose mentality and a stockpile of sophisticated manipulation weapons?[28]

Manipulation can be defined as the use of influence to have someone do something that may be against their own interests and that they would not do if they were well informed. Not all influence is manipulation: what counts is the *intention* behind the attempt to influence.

It's worth checking whether my own negotiation attitude is a healthy, non-manipulative one. If you believe that you don't manipulate, consider 'language for effect'. This term describes the use of words to have an emotional impact on someone else—a form of manipulation. For example, 'Do you know what time it is?' is often asked for effect.

I therefore suggest that, to avoid manipulation, I must:

- ☐ Assess my own intentions
- ☐ Assess my client's intentions
- ☐ Recognise manipulation and counter it.

Understanding outcomes, intentions and positions can help.

---

[28] I know of large companies that train their staff in Win–Lose negotiation techniques. It would be naive to deny the existence of this type of behaviour.

Outcomes, Intentions and Positions

As already stated, it makes sense in the context of a long-term, B2B relationship to aim for Win–Win negotiation *outcomes*.

Outcomes, Intentions and Positions		
Negotiation outcome	Win–Win	The contract satisfies needs and wants of both parties, who feel comfortable with it.
	Win–Lose	The contract satisfies needs and wants of one party only. The other feels that they obtained a poor deal.
	Lose–Lose	The contract satisfies neither party.
Negotiator's intentions with respect to other parties	Positive	The negotiator is prepared to make an extra effort to ensure that the opposite party gets something out of the deal—that they have a Win.
	Don't care	The negotiator does not care whether the other party feels they have a Win or not. They will not try to force them into a Lose position however.
	Neg've	The negotiator will not be satisfied unless they can push the other party into a Lose position.
Negotiator's position in general	OK/OK	The negotiator's outlook on life is a confident one. They believe in themselves (and their organisation) and are able to have confidence in others.
	OK/Not OK	The negotiator's outlook on life tends towards arrogance. They believe in themselves (and their organisation) but are sceptical about others' capabilities.
	Not OK/OK	The negotiator's outlook is timid. They lack confidence in themselves (and their organisation) and tend to think that others can do better than them.
	Not OK/Not OK	The negotiator's outlook is pessimistic. They believe neither in themselves, nor their organisation, nor in others.

In working with my client, I therefore need to understand whether they share my intention to achieve such an outcome. Is their *intention*, with respect to me, positive, negative, or don't they care about me, provided that they get what they want?

My client's general *position* with respect to others may influence their *intentions* with respect to me during the negotiation. This depends on their psychological make-up. For example, a person who is confident in themselves and has respect for and confidence in others can be said to have an OK/OK position. Someone who has confidence in themselves but no respect for or confidence in others has an OK/Not-OK position, and the two other combinations of OK and Not-OK are easy to guess.[29]

It can therefore be seen that outcomes, intentions and positions are described in similar ways, and that they may be correlated in many cases, but also that they are distinct concepts. They are summarised in the table opposite.

When negotiating, it is important to be able to judge whether a proposed solution will be Win–Win and also to assess the intentions of the parties involved. Understanding someone's position may be important if I have to deal with them on a repeated basis. This is because there tends to be a correlation between a person's position and their intentions, as can be appreciated by examining the table.

This last point notwithstanding, the concepts of outcome, intentions and position are quite orthogonal. It is quite possible to achieve a Win–Win outcome when faced with a negotiator who has 'don't care' intentions and an 'OK/Not-OK' position. It is even possible, I guess, to get to Win–Win when working with someone who has negative intentions and a 'Not-OK/Not-OK' position, but you would probably need a stiff drink afterwards.

Manipulation Techniques

The ability to recognise psychological ploys (which become manipulation techniques when used negatively) is extremely valuable in negotiation.

---

[29] See 'The OK Corral' in: Stewart & Joines : *TA Today—A New Introduction to Transactional Analysis* (StewartJoines 1987).

Kahneman (Kahneman 2013) explains that the brain works as though we have two systems. 'System 1' generates impressions, feelings and inclinations and operates automatically and extremely quickly. This is the system responsible for my reflexes when driving a car, my snappy reply when someone irritates me and my ability to instantly recognise the words on this page.

My 'System 2', on the other hand, is used for effortful mental activities, including complex computations. It is deliberate and, compared to System 1, relatively slow. I use it for analysing documents and writing computer programs, for example.

Though the existence of System 1 is explained by the logic of evolution, *it does not function according to logical principles*. It may be essential for survival but, logically speaking, it has many blind spots which may be targeted by manipulators.

One example is the phenomenon of anchors, already mentioned briefly in the discussion of Bottom Lines. Our brains cannot, it seems, ignore reference points that are presented to them, no matter how crazy they are. Kahneman gives the example of an experiment where, before being asked a question for which there was a numerical answer, people were asked to spin a wheel of fortune. They knew that the number corresponding to the point at which the wheel stopped had no meaning, but their answers were strongly biased by that number in any case (in fact, the wheel had been fixed to stop at one of two numbers, and the answers were pulled towards either one or the other).

As mentioned, anchoring, like all psychological ploys, exploits a blind spot in System 1. In a context where there are few references, any new one will have a huge biasing effect—we seem to need an anchor, any anchor, to cling on to.

Manipulation on the streets of San Francisco

I am reminded of two different street artists that I saw in San Francisco recently. At the end of their acts (which were completely independent —one was hip-hop and the other a crazy balancing act) both artists explained that they lived off of the generous donations of onlookers. Both of them also 'jokingly' mentioned that $100 would be a reasonable donation. $100 was their anchor!

Manipulative anchor or authoritative external reference?

If I am discussing the number of software licences that my client might need for next year, then they might point out that their team only uses five licences per year for software from another supplier (whereas I had been pushing them to take 12). If, upon further investigation, this reference turns out to be a reasonable one—the software is comparable and the numbers correct—then my client has used what is called an 'authoritative reference'. That is, a useful landmark, helping us to converge on an agreement.

On the other hand, if I find out that the software they are referring to is completely different from that being discussed and that its cost per licence is much lower, then there is a good chance that they are using this data manipulatively.

A second, common psychological ploy is framing. The classic example of this is describing a glass as being half-full or half-empty—the description is 'framed' to present either a positive or a negative view of a situation. Framing affects the way people feel and think about something primarily due to the way in which it is described. For example, the statements, '63 units failed' and '99.3 per cent of the units worked fine' may not have the same effect on an audience, even if the data behind the statements is identical. Again, this may be done for positive (enlightening) or negative (manipulative) reasons.

Kahneman explains, often in amusing terms, many different blind spots that our System 1s are susceptible to, and others have built on his work.

As mentioned, the key indicator when trying to understand whether I am facing a manipulator or am simply up against a skilled negotiator is their intention. Are they aiming for a Win–Win outcome or not? (As mentioned, a Win–Win negotiation result is possible even if one of the negotiators has a Win–Lose attitude, though it is harder to achieve.)

Of course, people cannot be relied upon to announce their real intentions, and so I have to look for clues as the conversation proceeds. Extensive Discovery, especially using the SUBROUTINE tool, helps unearth such clues. If a conversation ranges over many topics, and if Problems and Needs are given at least as much attention as Situations and Solutions, then the overall consistency (or lack of it) in my client's responses will inform me about their intentions.

Countering Manipulation with Meta-Communication

Meta-communication means discussing the process being used for a conversation, rather than its content. In other words, it is the technique of talking about a conversation at a level *above who said what*. Meta-communication is a powerful countermeasure against manipulation.

The reason can be seen from the definition of manipulation. As already discussed, influence becomes manipulation when used to make someone *unknowingly* act against their own interests. Once I have understood my would-be manipulator's ploy, then I am unlikely to do myself harm in this way, and by letting them know that I have understood their game—by meta-communicating —I will deter them from further manipulation attempts.

In response to 'It's got to be done by Friday!'
... rather than ask 'Why Friday?' or perhaps negotiate for a shift of the deadline until after the weekend, I could reply using meta-communication and say, 'Are you trying to put the pressure on?' In making this response, I go up a level and talk about motives for what my client just said, rather than staying at their communication level and talking about deadlines.

In fact, the value of meta-communication to CFEs goes way beyond its use in negotiation. Its benefits are similar to those of other types of abstraction and, since abstraction is practically the essence of engineering, CFEs should have no problem appreciating this. The Toolkit is, in a sense, an exercise in meta-communication, since it provides a level of abstraction for describing encounters. The ability to step back from conversations and describe them at this higher level is key to improving skills in the long term.

Countering the 'free' anchor with meta-communication

Having negotiated a good discount for my company's product a client suggests that, since they have no budget left, training be provided at no extra cost—i.e. free—even though it was not included in the price of the product. I decide that 'free' is a manipulative anchor. In other words, my client knows that training can't be provided for nothing and they are making this suggestion in order to push the cost down as much as possible.

In these circumstances, a sensible response, using meta-communication, might be: 'Frank, I can understand that you want to keep costs down but, honestly, this "no budget" thing sounds like a bit of a ploy to me. Let's put the training issue aside for the moment and focus on your technical support needs for the next two weeks ...'.

Notice that I don't respond directly to my client's suggestion. When using meta-communication, I work at a different level of abstraction, discussing the communication itself. Also, because my client has used an anchor, I try avoid further negotiation. This is so that the anchor cannot have its intended effect, which is to pull down the price of training.

In Brief

✦ By challenging clients, Customer-Facing Engineers can (1) protect themselves, their organisations and (ultimately) their clients from the consequences of unhealthy agreements, and (2) unlock possibilities that others have not seen.

✦ The SUBROUTINE and TMM tools give support for challenging. The practice also requires negotiation skill.

✦ CFEs negotiate a lot. Many situations require negotiation: time, resources and know-how are all negotiable items.

✦ The TABLE is a negotiation planning tool covering Exchanges, Fallbacks and Fallout for both parties, and also my Fall Lines.

✦ Fall Lines, which tell me when to pause and rethink, are helpful, whereas Bottom Lines are deprecated, since (1) they act like anchors and (2) they reduce my negotiation flexibility.

✦ In the context of long-term, B2B relationships, negotiations are generally multi-issue, involving time, money, people, etc.

✦ I use an interests-based approach, aiming at a Win–Win outcome, in the form of a contract (an agreement with actions).

✦ A contract may be written or verbal, explicit or secret.

✦ To be implementable, a contract must be manageable and motivational for all negotiation stakeholders.

✦ I observe the other negotiating party's intentions, which may be positive, uncaring or negative towards me.

✦ Negotiators must recognise manipulation techniques that can be used by people with negative intentions.

✦ Meta-communication provides a powerful counter to manipulation.

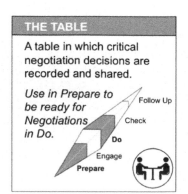

THE TABLE

A table in which critical negotiation decisions are recorded and shared.

Use in Prepare to be ready for Negotiations in Do.

Follow Up

Check

Do

Engage

Prepare

9. Writing Email: TWO-SECOND MESSAGE

*'I didn't attend the funeral, but I sent a nice email saying that
I approved of it',*
after Mark Twain[30]

The ambiguity in Mark Twain's note, above, was deliberate as well as humorous. Unfortunately, the same cannot be said of the ambiguities in millions of messages circulating around the workplace today.

Our effectiveness as Customer-Facing Engineers depends on communication and, of course, a significant part of it is done using email. To get an idea of just how significant this has become, let's have a look at some statistics.

A report from Radicati [31] shows that, on average, business users received 85 emails per day in 2014 (10 of which were spam), and that they produced 36. If the average amount of new text in an email is, say, 50 words, then this gives an average of 1,800 words per day.[32] For comparison, Stephen King recommends that writers aim for between 500 and 3,000 words per day when drafting a book, and his personal target is 2,000 (King 2000).

It seems that, like it or not, *we have all become professional writers.* I must therefore consider writing skills, and email writing technique in particular, to be one of my most important professional assets.

Unfortunately, it is not sufficient to refer to established texts on good writing practice in order to hone these skills. Reading, for example, Strunk and White's *The Elements of Style*[33] is an

---

[30] Of course, Mark Twain, 1835–1910, wrote 'letter', rather than 'email'.

[31] The Radicati Group 2014: I haven't found any third-party data to corroborate this report, but a glance at my own Email system shows that their data is credible.

[32] For example, on 18th August 2014, a day like any other, I wrote 1,277 new words in 24 mails. This is an average of 53.2.

[33] Strunk, WhiteKalman 2005: the book, the first edition of which was written in 1919, deliberately sidesteps the issue of writing email.

excellent way to improve my prose, but this is only one aspect of the modern problem. My task is to grab my audience's attention when they have 84 other emails to read, and when they might be using their computer, their phone or their tablet, perhaps sitting in their office, in an airport or in the bathroom. There are more things to consider than just prose.

Best writing practices are therefore evolving rapidly, and I think that this makes the present topic particularly interesting.

This chapter focuses on email composition, for spontaneous messages and replies, internal and external—it doesn't deal with the issue of managing large quantities of email, which is essentially a task management problem. For good ideas on the latter, please read, for example, Dave Allen's *Getting Things Done* (Allen 2001). This describes techniques for avoiding task overload, and incoming email is certainly a source of overload for many people.

This limitation in scope notwithstanding, I note that writing high-quality email, and knowing how to do so quickly, can lead to a significant reduction in workload (or to a significant increase in performance, which is another way of looking at things). Communication errors take time to sort out, whereas effective messages lead to prompt replies and quick results. Writing good email is one way of controlling my workload at its source.

The TWO-SECOND MESSAGE system, described here, was developed following requests from CFE managers in several companies that I work with. They pointed out that email is an essential tool of their trade, and that a lot of the specificity of the CFE role is therefore played out in email correspondence. Customer-Facing Engineers not only need to follow fundamental email guidelines that apply to everyone, but the detail of their work also mandates email practices that are specific to them. This chapter therefore starts with a review of email fundamentals before going on to describe the TWO-SECOND MESSAGE system and its CFE-specific aspects.

Goals

I suggest two goals to achieve when dealing with email:

1. Write email that is Nice and Clear.
2. Cope with email that is NOT Nice or NOT Clear.

To Write Email that is Nice and Clear

To ensure that my emails are 'nice and clear', I check that they are *difficult to misinterpret*.

This is because it's incredibly hard to judge the 'niceness' and 'clearness' of one's own efforts—I am blind to my faults (otherwise I wouldn't have so many). However, if I try to imagine the possible ways in which my mail could be *mis*understood, then I am focusing on the limitations of my audience, which is much easier to do.

To Cope with Email that is Nasty or Unclear

I must first identify nasty or unclear mails. Categorising them helps limit the surge of negative emotions that they might otherwise cause.

If an incoming message states 'You are clearly an incompetent, illiterate baboon ...', then, rather than getting annoyed and trying to refute this, it's best to treat the mail as I would a mosquito bite. Even if it hurts, the wound should not destabilise my whole being—I should be able to deal with it in an adult fashion. Of course, it can be hard to stay cool, and my immediate reaction may be anger, shame and depression. Once this has passed, however, simply labelling the mail as 'nasty/ unclear' enables me to deal with it effectively.

Above all, good emotional control will help me avoid making matters worse. Sometimes, a nasty/unclear email can present an opportunity to improve a relationship, but only if I stay in control. For example, if I see the need to confront a client in order to sort out a misunderstanding, then I could use the SUBROUTINE process described in Chapter 6. By categorising troublesome incoming mail as dispassionately as possible, I keep a clear head and can therefore exploit the tools and methods at my disposal.

Characteristics of the Email Channel

face2face	screen2screen	voice2voice	word2word	⬆ What you do
F2F	S2S	V2V	W2W	⬇ What you get
✔				Contextual information
✔				Physical view & contact
✔	✔			Facial expressions
✔	✔			Presentations & drawing
✔	✔	✔		Vocal clues
	✔		✔	Text
	rarely		✔	Permanent copy
			✔	Broadcast
live meeting	webex	telephone	letter, fax	
workshop	Skype		email, CRM	<- Examples
seminar			SMS, chat	

Alternative Communication Channels

Let's look at email's relationship with other forms of modern communication. The table above shows a continuum of possibilities, with the first four columns highlighting the 'features' of each of the encounter types.[34]

'Contextual information' means what can be learned from being in the same physical space as my clients—their offices or meeting rooms, for example. I notice people passing by, posters on the walls, the canteen facilities, etc. 'Physical view & contact' refers to the fact that my clients are right in front of me, emitting subtle, subliminal signals that would be eliminated by long-distance communication. 'Broadcast' refers to the facility with which word-to-word correspondence can be sent to many people at the same time. I hope that the other terms in the table are self-explanatory.

---

[34] CRM stands for Customer Relationship Management system, a web-based system that often integrates bug-tracking and which is used to communicate with and about customers in order to manage their commercial and support needs.

It is interesting to note that the richest communication environment is still the face-to-face meeting. In spite of modern technology, the best interpersonal connections use the same methods as in ancient Greece!

Notes on the Email Channel

The 'word2word' column is the only one with the 'Permanent copy' and 'Broadcast' features ticked. This tells me to be careful about what I include in email communication. Even if I am economical with copy lists, it doesn't stop others from forwarding my mail to whoever they like. Even if my intentions are pure and my message is not meant to offend, it doesn't stop someone from brooding over an interpretation that I haven't foreseen.

Second, the table shows that email keeps us disconnected from our clients—there are no ticks in the first five rows of the word2word column. However, email's transmission speed can fool us into thinking that we have a close connection to our correspondent. It may encourage the assumption that our client is more available than they really are, and this can lead to misunderstanding.

It is particularly important to manage one's expectations and assumptions when it comes to email response times. I am remote from my client, and even if I receive a reply from them within two minutes of sending a message, this tells me nothing about the importance they place on my message, their current availability, their mood, etc. While I may get excited by a quick reply and the possibility of wrapping up some business promptly, it could be that my next mail will be met with silence. What would this mean? Answer: probably nothing at all. For all I know, my client may have sent his first reply before leaving the office, walking out into the road and being run over by a bus!

Evolution has wired our brains to look for cause-and-effect relationships (without needing to understand the relationships). If my ancestors ate red berries then got sick, they stopped eating them. If they hadn't, then they would have died and not passed on their genes to me.

In the modern world, as a result of these genes, I see cause and effect relationships even where there are none. Hence, when I don't get the email response that I was hoping for, I try to link this 'effect' to the only causes in sight—either the content of my mail or myself (e.g. what does the client think of me and/or my company?). But I should not make assumptions based on email arrival times or on email non-arrival (unless my emails are systematically ignored over a long period). An important aspect of managing email is to have reasonable expectations for my client's response and to act rationally if there is none at all.

Having got my expectations in order, I am now in a position to take advantage of the TWO-SECOND MESSAGE system.

The TWO-SECOND MESSAGE (TSM)

The TWO-SECOND MESSAGE system is based upon the idea that, for an email to be effective, its purpose must become clear to the reader in just a couple of seconds. While this is not the only measure of effectiveness, its importance is emphasised by the 'TWO-SECOND MESSAGE' title, which is in itself a concise message.

The system is structured in order to (1) emphasise certain fundamentals, (2) highlight specific requirements of the CFE role, and (3) make it easy for users to produce customised guidelines that remain consistent with points (1) and (2). To this end, the fundamentals are expressed as a 'Think–Write–Pause' flow and a set of four general guidelines (under the heading 'GENERAL' in the diagram opposite). The CFE-specific part is captured in four sets of requirements (under the heading 'CFE-specific' in the diagram).

The Think–Write–Pause Flow

Think

This step describes the interval from the moment when an email is first envisaged to the moment when writing begins. This precious space of time can be used to save a great deal of work, pain and suffering.

The purpose of the Think step is to consider my email, whether it be the start of a thread or a reply, at a level above the

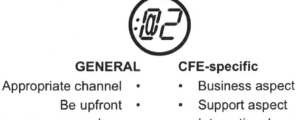

GENERAL	CFE-specific
Appropriate channel •	• Business aspect
Be upfront •	• Support aspect
Less is more, more or less •	• International
OK-ness •	• Internal

 Think–Write–Pause

> Detailed
> guidelines

detail of the words to be used. It gives me a chance to consider, for example:

- ▸ Will the email be a good investment of my time?
- ▸ Is email the appropriate communication channel?
- ▸ When replying, have I fully understood a received mail? Am I overreacting? Should I start a new thread? etc.

Write

This is the step where I hit the keys. Its purpose is obvious, and so I will not hit more keys than necessary here.

Pause

The Pause step is for checking and final reflection.

Things to be checked include the mundane, such as spelling and grammar, but also more delicate issues such as the copy list and any confidentiality issues. The pause, which can last from a split second to many hours, is my last opportunity to avoid sending something that was written while in, let's say, a suboptimal mood. A well-known problem with email is that the time from beginning to send is so short that there is no natural 'think it over' period. When we used to write things on paper, find stamps and so on, the pause imposed itself. These days, its existence depends on self-discipline.

General Guidelines

Appropriate Channel

Alternative communication channels were enumerated and discussed above. The first general guideline is to choose the one to use in an active way, rather than reverting to email out of habit or fear.

face2face	screen2screen	voice2voice	word2word	nothing	What you do
F2F	S2S	V2V	W2W	/dev/null	What you get
✔					Contextual information
✔					Physical view & contact
✔	✔				Facial expressions
✔	✔				Presentations & drawing
✔	✔	✔			Vocal clues
	✔		✔		Text
	rarely		✔		Permanent copy
			✔		Broadcast
live meeting	webex	telephone	letter, fax	n.a.	
workshop	Skype		email, CRM		<- Examples
seminar			SMS, chat		

It is a matter of common experience that some issues are better handled with a telephone call or a face-to-face meeting. If there is disagreement, then it may be tempting to stick with the security of an email, and to spend some time crafting justifications and arguments. However, as a quick look at the table above reminds us, email is not the best choice for delicate matters.

To reinforce this point, I have added a 'nothing' column to the table presented earlier, and labelled it '/dev/null' (sending data to the '/dev/null' device in Unix is a null operation). I was inspired to add the /dev/null channel by a thought-provoking blog from James Altucher, a serial entrepreneur (Altucher 2013). Entitled '*5 Ways to Do Nothing and be More Productive*', the blog suggests:

☐ Do nothing when you're angry

☐ Do nothing when you're paranoid

☐ Do nothing when you're anxious

☐ Do nothing when you're tired

☐ Do nothing when you want to be liked.

These points certainly apply when a nasty or unclear email has been received (in fact, the blog was triggered by such an event).

When I am overtaken by anger, paranoia, anxiety, etc., then I am no longer the cool, reliable professional that I would like to be. The key word here is *overtaken*. There is nothing wrong with feeling anger, paranoia, or any other emotion—it is impossible not to—but it's a bad idea to act while under the influence of such emotions. Just as it is unwise to do business when drunk, it is best to 'sober up' emotionally before replying to troublesome email (whether or not I use email for my reply).

Be Upfront

In keeping with the 'TWO-SECOND MESSAGE' title, my second general guideline is to be *upfront*. This has the double meaning of 'clear and forthright' and 'at the beginning'.

Messages should be written using straightforward language and organisation, and the most important part of the message must be towards the beginning (the front) of the text.

There are a number of tendencies to fight in order to be upfront:

▸ The story-telling tendency, where I start my tale at the chronological beginning and lead up to a climax (the main point).

▸ The 'stream of consciousness' tendency, where I write as I think, clarifying my thoughts to myself as I go, reaching my conclusion (the main point) at the end.

▸ The 'this mail took ages to write, and I am going to make absolutely sure that you read all of it' tendency, where I deliberately put my main point at the end of the message in order to force the reader to fight their way through the whole thing.

Mails exhibiting these tendencies irritate readers. Having fallen into the trap of reading them once, they will not want to repeat the experience and may ignore future mails from the same source. Hence the need to:

- ☐ Help the reader to decide quickly: read, file or trash?
- ☐ Indicate straight away if the mail is just for information
- ☐ Make any request for action at the start of the mail
- ☐ In replies, express any agreement or refusal at the start.

The body of the mail can elaborate, if necessary.

Getting your email read

To: CFEs everywhere

Subject: Getting your email read

An email's first sentence is as important as its title.

Many people decide what email to *open* based on the identity of the sender alone. They then decide whether to *read* it based on the first few words seen. Mobile devices often display just the first few words of each message, to allow the user to do such filtering.

Of course, the title is still a useful thing, especially for browsing and searching.

Please let me know if you have comments or questions.

Regards,

...

Less is More, More or Less

Short is good, but too short is cryptic. For example, '<=>, >|<' is shorthand for 'less is more, more or less', but I can read the latter text more quickly.

Hence, while trying to keep emails as short and simple as possible, it is important to avoid excessive, counterproductive brevity. With this in mind, I should:

- ☐ Use white space generously (blank lines mainly)
- ☐ Separate concerns, to facilitate speed-reading, e.g.:
  - ☐ Put each idea in a separate paragraph

☐ Keep facts and opinions apart

☐ Put questions in one place, information in another.

Similarly, minimising the complexity of grammar will help the reader. When writing English, for example:

☐ The active, 'subject, verb, object', style is preferred (e.g. 'Someone deleted the file' is better than 'The file was deleted by someone').

☐ The present tense is preferred (many languages use the present for almost everything).

☐ Long sentences should be broken up, to avoid more than one subordinate clause. Not only are multiple subordinate clauses difficult to understand, but they can take longer to write. Try writing this bullet point as a single sentence to see what I mean!

OK-ness

Once an email has been written, I must check three things:

☐ Is the email OK?

  ☐ Are the facts right, the dates correct, etc.?

  ☐ Are the grammar, formatting and spelling right?

  ☐ Are the cited attachments attached?

☐ Am I OK?

  ☐ Do I feel comfortable with the email content?

  ☐ Will sending it cause me to worry about how it will be received, or to start anxiously waiting for a response?

☐ Will the intended recipients be OK?

  ☐ Could the email cause them extra work or stress?

  ☐ Is email the best channel and is this the right moment?

Having made these checks, I can hit the 'send' button and stop thinking about that particular communication. My mind is freed up to focus on other things.

If I need a reply to my email before a certain date then a good way to get this off my mind is to use my personal organisation system. By setting an alarm, I can afford to forget about the pending reply until it's due.

CFE-Specific Requirements

It's easy to spot skilled Customer-Facing Engineers by looking at their email writing style. Not only do they write Nice and Clear messages, as discussed earlier, but they also use tactics that:

▸ Favour an enduring business relationship

▸ Simplify and accelerate technical discussions

▸ Respectfully take into account cultural and geographical differences

▸ Do the above equally well for internal and external clients.

In brief, a CFE-specific style for writing email will capture many of the principles that have been discussed already in this book, in a form that is appropriate to email. The following section gives examples of how this can be achieved.

Detailed, Customisable Guidelines

The following guidelines are examples that can be derived by combining the TSM's four general guidelines and the four CFE-specific requirements with the 'Think–Write–Pause' flow. Such guidelines are generally developed for CFE teams, and preferences will depend on the nature of the team's work. Field teams have a slightly different viewpoint from CFE teams based in a head office, for example, and CFEs supporting software are faced with different problems from those supporting hardware.

I know some CFE teams that, because of the highly sensitive nature of the intellectual property that they handle, have to include legal disclaimers in every mail sent. Similarly, companies that work in the area of Aerospace and Defence have strict guidelines that are specific to their domains.

Although I haven't made much of it here, some guidelines are more applicable to email that starts a new thread than to replies. When a client sends me a list of questions, the structure of my reply may be driven by their original email (e.g. sometimes the best way to deal with it is to interlace my answers with their questions in the reply text). Such exceptions are left to the reader's good judgement, though, if they are important, a team may decide to make them the subject of specific guidelines.

Think

T1. WIIFM

What's in it for me? Is this worth my time?

T2. Choose the channel

Consider communication options other than email—e.g. telephone or tele/video conference. When replying to email, question the reflex of replying to one email with another.

T3. Decide who to put or keep on copy

Be careful with who is on copy. If in doubt, ask—there is no safe option by default. Both too many and too few Cc:s can be dangerous, depending on the circumstances. As well as asking (e.g. by telephone), another possibility is to make it clear in the mail that you have left it to your client to copy the mail to the appropriate people in their organisation.

When replying to a mail, don't automatically maintain the original copy list. Keep the list to the minimum necessary.

Is your colleagues' privacy protected? Think carefully before putting them on open copy to people outside your organisation.

T4. Think positive

Adopt positive beliefs about your clients' capabilities. Avoid the pastime of ridiculing them with your colleagues. By having a positive mindset with respect to your clients you increase the chances that your communication will be respectful and constructive.

T5. Be careful with confidential information

If in doubt, leave it out (or ask). If your company has confidentiality guidelines, then refer to them as necessary.

T6. Acknowledge receipt of support requests promptly

Even if a support request can't be answered immediately, it should be acknowledged. This point notwithstanding, a little delay before investing in a detailed reply can act as a low pass filter, reducing the total volume of email traffic and allowing time for spurious problems to sort themselves out.

T7. Beware of assumptions

Don't assume that your client understood or remembered all the points in your last mail. Imagine that they read it while distracted. Consider reiterating important points, just to be sure.

Be sure that you have fully understood an incoming issue before replying to it. If there is any doubt, ask for clarification. Try to avoid sending any information with the request for clarification, as this can confuse.

T8. What about the Support Case system?

Has all relevant mail been copied into the Support Case system? Is there anything in there that might help with the issue in question?

Write

W1. Respect the thread

When replying, don't alter the mail title unless absolutely necessary.

W2. Simple formatting

Don't rely on rich text, html or other formatting. Your client's tools may be different from yours, with unexpected consequences.

W3. Write upfront email

State your purpose/main message clearly, immediately after the greeting.

W4. Structure long emails as a head and a tail

If a mail must be long, break it down into a short header that includes the sign-off (preceded by any Next Steps) and a longer tail or attachment.

W5. Use playback

As for face-to-face meetings, if you reword what your client has written it can reassure them that you have understood. It could also prevent a misunderstanding.

W6. Clear Next Steps

Ensure that Next Steps (e.g. a request for information in a reply) are clearly visible and likely to be read (see the W4 guideline on breaking long emails down into a header and a tail).

W7. Discovery checklist

For support work with a repetitive element, maintain a checklist of questions that you frequently need answers to—see examples below:

- Discover the client's intent—what are they trying to do?
- Discover the last thing that worked before the problem arose.
- Discover tool versions, environment, etc.

W8. Explain the process

If you cannot solve an issue immediately, explain the process that you are using to do so and give the client some idea of when you will get back to them next.

W9. Help them to help you

Send clear instructions on how to capture examples etc. If possible, send scripts or similar to help with this.

W10. Refer to and reply

Refer to existing documentation if possible, *as well as* replying to the issue. You should still reply to the issue in the email, even if it simply means copy-and-paste from the document that you reference. The client will perhaps realise that they should have looked in the documentation before contacting you next time, and they will appreciate your courtesy.

W11. Stick to the problem in hand

Make sure that explanations and examples don't go beyond what is necessary to solve the problem. Don't show off—at least, not in the reply to an issue. If there is interesting, supplementary information to send to a client, then make this the subject of a separate communication.

W12. Take care of the greeting

For example, when you email someone after a gap, or when switching to email from some other form of communication, a few words of consideration can help: e.g. 'I hope that this email finds you well', 'Thank your for time on the telephone earlier'. High-context cultures (e.g. Japan, China) expect this sort of consideration more than low-context ones (e.g. USA, Israel), where a more direct approach is normal.

In a technical support context, it is normal to address people by their first name in mail. However, this also depends on culture. For example, you should use <surname>-san with Japanese correspondents, even if they sign their mails with their first names.

W13. Avoid irritating phrases

Avoid phrases such as 'as I explained previously' or 'as you will see from my previous mail'—that sort of thing can be interpreted as rude and/or as an accusation.

W14. Thanks

Thank the client if appropriate (e.g. for raising a real issue, since this helps you improve the product).

W15. Time zones

When organising a meeting across time zones, state the times explicitly in all the time zones concerned. Don't rely on calendar invitations to do this automatically—they don't always work.

Pause

P1. Possible to misunderstand?

How could your mail be *mis*understood? Is there any humour in the mail? If so, is it appropriate for all possible readers? Are emoticons used to indicate intent?

P2. Attachments

Are they of a reasonable size? If they are referred to, are they really attached? If they are attached, are they referred to?

P3. Address lists OK?

Beware of the autocomplete feature on email tools: double-check the address lists.

A common convention is that 'To:' means *for action/ attention*, 'Cc:' means *for information only* and 'Bcc:' means *for your private information, do not forward*.

P4. Spell check

Is the spelling OK?

P5. Quote level?

Is the quote level no higher than three?

Avoid excessive quoting. This often occurs in messages that are answered point by point, with the question–answer session visible through different quote levels. Beyond three levels of quote, reformat and start again … or maybe pick up the telephone.

P6. Feeling OK about sending this, really?

How do you feel? Don't hit the 'send' button if you are feeling irritated, even if you think that your mail is polite. Do you really need to send the mail this minute, or could you wait for an hour (and perhaps use the time to recheck it or get a second opinion)?

Examples

Some of the following examples come from the world of circuit design and semiconductors. However, even if you work in another domain, I believe that you will understand them easily.

Concerning a Client's Technical Problem

A brief email, but too brief

Comments on this mail are indicated in [square brackets].

Cc: another AE , another client engineer, AE manager [1]

Subject: Re: ACT problems

Hi Tony,

from the analysis of the clock tree I did so far, I would say the clock tree is ok [2]. It seems that the clock skew reporting in best case doesn't work correctly. I can't reproduce that the clock tree insertion stops at clock gating cells, but I used a clock tree browser of a higher version. To be sure I checked the fanout of the clock gating cells with 2 different ways, and I can't find any problem. But I will investigate the reported results and will do a request to fix the clock tree reporting. [3]

Do you have the possibility to check the clock tree in a different tool, to be on the safe side.[4][5]

Regards,

Frank

171

[1]: See guideline T3 on copy lists. Also, given this list, it is all the more important that the email text be easy to scan for important information.

[2]: It wouldn't have hurt to start the sentence with a capital letter!

[3]: Less is more, *more or less*. By trying to keep the mail short and compact, the writer has compressed too much into one paragraph, which is tough to read. There are three ideas in this paragraph, and each should be in a separate one: the analysis, what the engineer has done (checking with a higher version of the software) and what he will do next.

[4]: Is this a question (there is no question mark), or a request? It is probably the latter, but the sentence is not clear enough, and the writer doesn't say whether he is expecting an immediate answer.

[5]: This is probably the most important point in the mail—a request for action—and so it should go at the start (see guideline W3).

Improved version
Hi Tony,

I am writing with the results of my analysis so far, and to ask you to do another test yourself.

If it is possible—please let me know—could you check the clock tree in a different tool? This could help us to close this case faster.

From the analysis of the clock tree I did so far, I would say that the tree itself is ok. However, it seems that the clock skew reporting in best case doesn't work correctly. If confirmed, then this is a bug (see below).

You reported that the clock tree insertion stops at clock gating cells. I have not been able to reproduce this behaviour. However, it may be because I used a different (and later) version of the clock tree browser from you. In fact, I checked the fanout of the clock gating cells in 2 different ways, but couldn't find any problem.

I am now taking the following actions:

1. Further investigation of the results that you reported. I will report back to you on this tomorrow.

2. *Requesting a fix for the clock tree reporting (support case #1234).*

I will look out for your reply concerning the use of a different tool.

Thanks and Regards

Frank

A Complaint from a CFE to an Internal Group

Irritating

Comments on this mail are indicated in [square brackets], and elaborated after the mail text.

Subject: Re: Case # 00183767 is now closed

Ben, Sally,

It is embarrassing to bury this CR with no ceremony. [1]

This is a feature Sally told the customer already exists in the tool and could be easily exposed to the user.

Sally: You told this to Amit at lunch during the meeting here in Munich. Since then, he asks me about it nearly every day! [2] *Beside that, I believe this is a very useful feature that will help users produce their custom post-signoff flow and spare some Change Requests on Ben :)*

Best regards, [3]

Alex

[1]: See guideline W3, 'Write upfront mail'. What's the purpose of this mail?

[2]: See guideline W13, 'Avoid irritating phrases'. The phrase 'you told this ...' and the strength of 'nearly every day!' ('often' would do) could irritate.

[3]: I suggest that this mail violates the general guideline on OK-ness. In spite of the smiley and the 'Best regards', the mail contains an accusation ('you told this ...') and lacks a constructive suggestion. I wouldn't feel comfortable sending it, as I wouldn't know how the recipients might react.

Improved version

Subject: Re: Case # 00183767 is now closed

Ben, Sally,

I am writing because I am embarrassed about this Change Request and, frankly, don't know what to say to my customer (see below). I would be grateful either for your suggestions, or for your help to get it moving again.

When in Munich, Sally mentioned to the customer that the feature in question exists in the tool and could be easily exposed to the user. Since then, he has asked me about it several times.

Besides that, I believe this is a very useful feature that will help users produce their custom post-signoff flow and spare some Change Requests on Ben :)

Please can you let me know your ideas?

Thanks and Best Regards ...

An Invitation to a Technical Training Course

Confusing

Subject: XYZ Professional Applications, 16–18 June

We're pleased to invite you to attend the XYZ Professional Applications programme.

As you are aware, the company is looking to achieve significant growth over the next five years and our applications teams will be pivotal in delivering this success. The purpose of this advanced-level, 3-day course (supported by targeted eLearning plans) is to ensure that we all are able to access the best methodologies, tools and skills for the customers we are working with and are united as a team in securing the support we need from the rest of the organisation. The course description, attached, will give you more information on the course content.

The course is being held in San Jose (the exact location will be confirmed ASAP) and it will be led by Viktor Bakoff, who some of you will have met at our recent Sales Conference.

Ahead of the training you will need to complete some pre-learning; this includes two short videos and a short self-assessment test. These, together, will take no more than 30 minutes to complete.

9. Writing Email: TWO-SECOND MESSAGE

To access the eLearning system, select the Tools option on the front page of the intranet and select 'e-learn'.

If you are accessing the system for the first time, your log in details are (for example):

Username: firstname_surname

Password: welcome (you will be asked to change this when you log on)

Please note you will need to have the latest version of Java installed on your computer in order to run the software. If you are directed to the Java website please contact the IT service desk on x 7356 who can install this for you.

Once you have accessed the eLearning home screen, click on 'View Learning Plan'. The learning plan that has been selected for you is called 'Global Apps Programme (Pre-Learning)'.

If you experience any difficulty logging into the system, or need any other support, please contact Hector Humdrum at hector@...

Please note, the training hours for each day are as follows:

Days 1 and 2: 0830–1800 [Refreshment breaks: 1030–1045; 1230–1330; 1530–1545]

Day 3: 0830–1530 [Refreshment breaks: 1030–1045; 1200–1300]

If you have any questions about the course, please don't hesitate to speak to me or to Billy Spiggot.

Best regards ...

This email has a problem of structure—I suggest that it violates guideline W4, 'Structure long emails as a head and a tail'. See also the general guideline 'Less is more', which includes advice on separating different ideas into different parts of the email.

The mail makes good use of white space, and all the information in it is expressed in clear sentences. However, at a higher level, it would benefit from an organisation that separated (1) the purpose of the course, (2) the actions requested, (3) information about the course, and (4) information needed to carry out the actions requested.

Improved version

Subject: For action please—XYZ Professional Applications course

We're pleased to invite you to attend the XYZ Professional Applications programme.

In the mail that follows I will (1) explain the purpose of the course and (2) ask you to do certain preparatory work. You will also find, in the attachments:

* Logistical information about the course

* An official course description

* Instructions on the use of the eLearning system (needed for prep.).

As you are aware, the company is looking to achieve significant growth over the next five years and our applications teams will be pivotal in delivering this success. The purpose of this advanced-level, 3-day course (supported by targeted eLearning plans) is to ensure that we all are able to access the best methodologies, tools and skills for the customers we are working with and are united as a team in securing the support we need from the rest of the organisation.

Ahead of the training you will need to complete some pre-learning; this includes two short videos and a short self-assessment test. These, together, will take no more than 30 minutes to complete—see attached instructions.

If you have any questions about the course, please don't hesitate to speak to me or to Billy Spiggot.

Best regards ...

ATTACHMENT 1: Course logistics.

The course is being held in San Jose from 16th to 18th June (the exact location will be confirmed ASAP) and it will be led by Viktor Bakoff, who some of you will have met at our recent Sales Conference.

The training hours for each day are as follows:

Days 1 and 2: 0830–1800 [Refreshment breaks: 1030–1045; 1230–1330; 1530–1545]

Day 3: 0830–1530 [Refreshment breaks: 1030–1045; 1200–1300]

ATTACHMENT 2: Official course description (a Word file, not shown)

ATTACHMENT 3: eLearning instructions

To access the eLearning system, select the Tools option on the front page of the intranet and select 'e-learn'.

If you are accessing the system for the first time, your login details are (for example):

Username: firstname_surname

Password: welcome (you will be asked to change this when you log on)

Please note you will need to have the latest version of Java installed on your computer in order to run the software. If you are directed to the Java website please contact the IT service desk on x 7356, who can install this for you.

Once you have accessed the eLearning home screen, click on 'View Learning Plan'. The learning plan that has been selected for you is called 'Global Apps Programme (Pre-Learning)'.

If you experience any difficulty logging into the system, or need any other support, please contact Hector Humdrum at hector@...

In Brief

✦ The name of the TWO-SECOND MESSAGE (TSM) system reminds us that the purpose of a well-written mail should be clear to the reader within two seconds.

✦ A detailed, customised set of email guidelines can be produced by combining the TSM's four general guidelines and the four CFE-specific requirements and its 'Think–Write–Pause' flow.

✦ The TSM's general guidelines are (1) appropriate channel, (2) be upfront, (3) less is more, more or less and (4) OK-ness.

✦ Its CFE-specific requirements concern (1) the business relationship, (2) the support aspect, (3) the international aspect and (4) considerations for the CFE's own organisation.

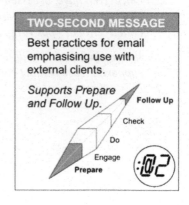

10. Getting Help and Collaboration: OAR

'What do I do when bugs won't go away?
(Does it worry you to be alone?)
How do I feel by the end of the day?
(Are you sad because you're on your own?)
No, I get by with a little help from my friends
Mm I get high with a little help from my friends
Mm going to try with a little help from my friends',
The Beatles (slightly modified)

The focus of this book has generally been on external clients, even though I have mentioned the applicability of its content to internal clients too. It is important that Customer-Facing Engineers communicate effectively with colleagues in their parent organisations since, without a little help from their friends, they will not be able to assist their external clients.

In fact, one of the biggest dilemmas of a Customer-Facing Engineer is that, at the moment of committing to clients, they can't be sure of how much backup they will get from their parent organisation, even though help is available in principle. This concerns many different kinds of help: bug fixes, advice, visits, demonstrations, presentations, materials, budget, etc. No matter what the need, the ability to influence managers and peers is essential to getting help and collaboration.

The nature of this challenge varies considerably according to the way in which a CFE's parent organisation is structured, and on where they fit into the structure. People who work exclusively in the field, perhaps thousands of kilometres from a company office and spending much more time with their customers than with colleagues, have a different view from those situated in company offices and labs. Hence, generalisations can be misleading.

I travel extensively in my work with field teams, and I have come across all sorts of combinations: head offices in Europe with CFEs in the USA and Asia, and vice versa; field teams that are independent of any business unit and others that are tightly attached; CFEs that belong to technical organisations and others that belong to sales or marketing organisations; and so on.

The common theme is that, at some time or another, all CFEs are faced with the difficulty of obtaining help from people in their parent organisation *who don't report directly to them*. They ask for help, often by email, but the response time does not meet their expectations (to put it politely). A frequent complaint is that people in their parent organisations don't understand the constraints associated with work in the field. Funnily enough, the objects of this complaint often feel that their difficulties are poorly understood also.

In brief, there are sometimes (1) challenges caused by a CFE's lack of control over resources, and (2) frustrations all round due to the difficulty that each collaborator has in envisaging the situation of the other.

This chapter can offer no miracle cures, but it will suggest a non-intuitive approach to these problems that is inherently safe and potentially very advantageous. It may provide an original and promising new strategy for CFEs faced with the frustrations just described.

The OAR Tool

> *'If you want to build a ship, don't assemble your men and women and give them orders, nor explain to them each detail, nor tell them where to find each thing. If you want to build a ship, have a passion for the sea grow in their hearts'*,[35]
> Antoine de Saint-Exupéry (aviator and writer)

The ICON9® tools seen so far will help me to plan and execute encounters with colleagues, to confront them in a non-conflictual way and to manage written (email) conversations. However, as Saint-Exupéry points out in the quote above, there is more to getting help and

---

[35] Original text (Saint-Exupéry 1948):Créer le navire ce n'est point tisser les toiles, forger les clous, lire les astres, mais bien donner le goût de la mer qui est un, et à la lumière duquel il n'est plus rien qui soit contradictoire mais communauté dans l'amour.

collaboration than simply being efficient. I have to motivate these colleagues, and the OAR tool prepares me for discussions that will do this. It stands for:

- ❏ **Our challenge**—looking beyond the immediate objectives for this encounter.

- ❏ **Audience** information, anticipated questions, concerns and related data on the *external* client.

- ❏ **Resources** that will allow my internal client to plan.

To understand how OAR is used, the following example starts with a MAP-based approach to preparing an *internal* meeting:

Preparation for a meeting to request help

My objectives = get help from the Product Engineers for the JFuse problem at ACME

Audience = Harry, the Product Engineering Manager (a busy person who regularly receives requests like this from CFEs)

Plan = OAR, PAGE, discover Harry's position, explain my situation, ask for help

---

Having written this MAP, which prepares me for the meeting with my *internal* client, I now proceed with the first point of my plan, which is to think through the three points of OAR. The relationship between the use of MAP and OAR in this case is therefore:

OAR helps me to adopt a particular mindset[36] when I approach Harry for help. It takes account of the fact that he and I are neither strangers—since we work for the same organisation—nor are we close colleagues: most of the time we work on different short-term objectives in worlds that are far apart. It is *my* objective to support ACME, not Harry's, even though supporting external clients may be one of the general objectives that he has agreed with his management. Since we have a peer-to-peer relationship, I can't simply delegate my work to him, and I must assume that he will listen to me then decide on his own priorities.

So, rather than simply hitting him directly with My objectives, I think first about a higher-level objective that we share —Our challenge. To do this, I look beyond my immediate objective, which, in this case, is to find a resolution to the JFuse bug. The objective behind this—let's label it 'level N+1'—is to maintain a positive image with my customer, ACME. At the next level up (N+2), my objective is to further develop business with the company, since they are a reference account in my region, Southern Europe. Going up one more level (N+3), my objective is to displace our main competitor in this region and become the dominant supplier. This is also, as it happens, a strategic priority of my company, and so Harry is driven by it too.

Our challenge is, therefore, to crack the Southern European market. To do that, we have to win ACME over, and fixing the JFuse bug quickly would make a great impression. Harry, could you help?

Of course, if he is going to be able to assist, Harry will need information, especially on the beneficiaries of the work. This is why the A of OAR stands for Audience. The client remains at the heart of our concerns, and my colleague needs to have as much information about them as possible.

Finally, Harry needs to understand what I expect him to do. Or does he? My free-spirited colleague may not appreciate being micromanaged through the work. He will probably have his own ideas on how to achieve our aims, even if he needs my assistance on some aspects. Hence, rather than suggesting a plan, I should let

---

[36] That is, a systemic mindset, discussed in a later section of this chapter.

him know what Resources (the R of OAR) are available, then leave him to do his own planning. This respects his autonomy and allows him to work my request into his other priorities.

Let's look at OAR's three components in more detail.

Our Challenge

The objectives stack

When attempting to formulate my objectives as a challenge, I find it helpful to think in terms of an 'objectives stack'. Every objective hides an ulterior objective, which I have called the 'N+1' objective. For example, if my objective is to find the cause of a software bug, my N+1 objective may be to get a piece of engine-control software running. My N+2 objective could be to have a road demonstration ready by Friday. The N+3 objective might be to impress X with our new injection control capabilities, and so on. By working through this objectives stack, I can usually find a level that represents a challenge that my colleague could readily associate with.

The OAR tool embodies a *systemic* approach, to be discussed in a later section. The emphasis on higher-level objectives is consistent with such an approach.

Influence versus delegation

I prepare for a meeting using OAR because I need to influence my internal client—to persuade them to assist me.

If I were a manager, then I could perhaps delegate support problems to someone reporting to me. While a manager certainly has to motivate his collaborators when passing work to them, there is a clear difference between the situation of a CFE asking their peers or management for help and that of a manager delegating work someone that reports to them. Motivated or not, a collaborator is likely to accept the task that is assigned, and to give it the priority that the manager suggests (perhaps for this reason, the literature on delegation puts a lot of emphasis on describing objectives clearly—e.g. SMART[37]— rather than persuasively).

---

[37] SMART is a checklist and stands for Specific, Measurable, Agreed, Realistic and Time-based. There are some variations on the acronym.

Influence versus manipulation

Many engineers associate any attempt to persuade or influence with manipulation, believing that the facts should speak for themselves. People who make this association generally believe, therefore, that the only honest way to make a request is to present one's case clearly, without embellishment.

This viewpoint is based on a preference for logic as a means to resolve issues. Unfortunately, the logic of the argument is itself flawed. If I were to present my argument to a computer, then I would agree that a 'facts only' approach would be best. When arguing with people, however, it is important to understand that emotion drives decisions also. Countless psychological studies have demonstrated that even people who pride themselves on their rational approach are, in fact, strongly influenced by their emotions when making decisions (for example: Guillaud 2011).

As mentioned in Chapter 8, the difference between influence and manipulation lies in the intentions of the influencer. If I limit myself to scientific fact alone, then my influence will simply be less than if I also use methods that appeal to the emotions. By associating a request for help with a challenge that is likely to engage my colleague, rather than simply with an immediate objective that I need help with, I am certainly trying to influence them. However, providing that I don't hide my own motives or deliberately underplay the commitment required from them, then I am not being manipulative.

Helping colleagues buy into the challenge

As discussed, the task in hand is bound to be important for our organisation at some level (the N+1, 2, etc. objectives). Maybe long-term business will be affected, or there is an opportunity to do something that the organisation has never done before, or perhaps we have the chance to publicly outshine our competition, or whatever. In asking for assistance with something that is perhaps urgent and short-term, I also *must share my enthusiasm for these higher-level objectives.* 'I need some help to debug an 800-line customer script' is unlikely to get my colleague's pulse racing. 'We need some help with EasySpace. Do you remember that we worked with them on their Mars lander? They need some help with a new project …' is more likely to get them engaged.

Everyone needs (and some people crave) visibility, and CFEs often make requests to engineers who are buried deeply in their organisations. These people can be doing great jobs but, since they are not as close to the 'front line' as CFEs, their work may go unnoticed by customers and executives, for example. By *ensuring* 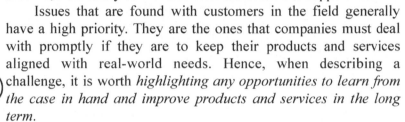 *that my colleagues' contributions are given the visibility they deserve*, I am likely to increase their motivation to support me.

Issues that are found with customers in the field generally have a high priority. They are the ones that companies must deal with promptly if they are to keep their products and services aligned with real-world needs. Hence, when describing a challenge, it is worth *highlighting any opportunities to learn from the case in hand and improve products and services in the long term.*

The interface with the outside world is linked to all three of the points just mentioned. Ultimately, this interface affects everyone in the company, and so it interests them. By making a clear link between what I am requesting (e.g. a product fix, a software upgrade, a few slides) and the ultimate reason for my request (e.g. a trade show, a customer production issue, a safety or security problem), I therefore make it easier for my colleagues to see a challenge rather than a hassle.

Sounding natural and realistic

Were I to burst into a colleague's office and announce, 'Our challenge, Jenny, is to win back the Gizmo market from the dark forces of MachoCorp!', then people might start to avoid me.

I wrote above, 'The OAR tool prepares me for discussions [with colleagues] …', and the words *'prepares me'* are important. The tool does not give me a formula for manipulating colleagues. Rather, it helps me to get my thinking on the right level before I get into conversation with them.

Thanks to this preparation, the discussion itself will use everyday language and sound quite natural. The words 'Our challenge' are unlikely to be used and the challenge may not even be spoken of explicitly—it could become part of a secret contract with my colleague, as discussed in Chapter 8. The crucial thing is to have a discussion at a level where collaboration is more likely than resistance.

Audience

> *'Forget your generalized audience. In the first place, the nameless, faceless audience will scare you to death and in the second place [...] it doesn't exist. In writing, your audience is one single reader. I have found that sometimes it helps to pick out one person [...] and write to that one',*
> John Steinbeck (Steinbeck 1975)

Steinbeck's advice may have been aimed at writers, but we can learn from the emphasis that it places on envisaging the audience. If I do not provide my colleague with such a focus, then I am leaving them to imagine all kinds of fictitious needs, and they could end up not knowing where to start the requested work. Alternatively, they could go ahead but not know when to stop!

Hence when asking a colleague for support, I need to pay particular attention to the 'Audience' aspect of the request, so that:

▸ My colleague understands the Audience and their needs

▸ I am not perceived as the beneficiary of the work, but as a facilitator (i.e. I am not confused with the Audience).

My colleague will probably be more motivated by the prospect of helping an external customer than by the idea of working on my behalf. Hence, it may be desirable to establish a direct line of communication between my internal and external clients, although this is not always the case. In fact, it may go against my internal client's need to keep a certain distance from customers, to avoid being swamped by direct requests from them. Of course, one of the roles of a CFE is to protect their internal clients in this sense.

In summary, it is my responsibility to convey an accurate picture of the end customer (the Audience) for whatever work I am asking to have done, and to facilitate any communication between my internal and external clients in a way that respects their needs.

Resources

The final piece of information that my colleague needs, once they have understood the challenge and the beneficiary, is what they have to work with. Before I address my colleague, I must therefore review the resources that I can make available to them. There are a number of important benefits to be gained by doing this:

CHECKLIST

- ☐ *Eureka/Of course!* Bringing to mind all the resources that my colleague may be able to use may make me think of something that I had previously overlooked. Before talking to my colleague, I could perhaps try something else ...

- ☐ *Respect our peer–peer relationship.* While I want to be as helpful as possible, I must not interfere with my colleague's way of working. It's up to them to decide how to go about fixing the bug, preparing the presentation, or whatever it is I have requested. OAR's emphasis on 'Resources', rather than 'Plan', reminds me of this.

- ☐ *Encourage other resource ideas.* By going to the trouble of identifying the resources available to my colleague, I may prompt them to think of other things that they need.

- ☐ *Preclude excuses.* If I provide my colleague with everything that they need (including a number to call in case of problems) then I make it hard for them to wriggle out of any obligations that they may make. This is not manipulation ... it's just an insurance scheme.

If I compare OAR with MAP, the 'Resources' part is a kind of 'anti-Plan'. It reminds me that I do not have complete control over how the end result will be achieved (hence, I cannot plan the steps to achieving it), but I can still encourage a favourable outcome by stimulating the system with the right inputs. This is consistent with a systemic approach, described below.

OAR in Practice

The following example is as close as we can get, in the context of a book, to a live use of OAR:

ICON9 network project

Our challenge

I envisage a network of engineers motivated to excel both in customer-facing work and in general, interpersonal communication. The circular dependency between these two capabilities is a natural source of energy and inspiration for this project.

Such a network can make a small but significant contribution to communication culture in the widest sense, since miscommunication is one of the greatest dangers for our world. Many writers have observed that the technical revolution is outpacing social evolution.

Notice that the suggested challenge goes well beyond the immediate objective of learning the ICON9 tools.

Audience

Although the people concerned by our immediate efforts are customers and colleagues, we can extend this audience to other situations: an interview with the bank manager, negotiating with a teenage daughter for access to the bathroom ... there are plenty of occasions for practice. Some of the tools—particularly the TWO-SECOND MESSAGE and the SUBROUTINE—are useful in all walks of life. Others are more professionally oriented. I don't recommend using the Encounter Process on a first date, for example!

Resources

The ICON9 system provides an initial structure for this project, and the ICON9.net web pages a place to find information and contacts.

Notice that this statement leaves the reader free to choose their own way to take up the challenge, should they wish to. There is no 'how to' element in the statement.

Of course, I would not normally show my OAR preparation to someone that I was meeting—you are seeing it here because of the special context of reading a description of OAR itself. For an encounter where I used OAR for preparation, I would review the three points to myself so that they are fresh in my mind before meeting my client.

The Systemic Approach

Knowing where to tap the system

A complex machine isn't working and an expert is summoned to fix it.

After evaluating the situation for a few minutes, the expert whips out a hammer and gives the machine a light tap. The machine starts right up.

When the expert's bill for €1,000 arrives, he is asked to itemise and explain the charge. He replies: Hitting the machine with a hammer: €5. Knowing where to hit it: €995.

Definition

The OAR tool supports a systemic approach to problems, rather than the analytical one used for most engineering activities. In the case of the expert and the complex machine (Berne 1963), above, an analytical approach would involve a study of each component of the system, in a bid to find the faulty part. This would make sense for a simple machine, with few components, interconnections and feedback loops, and where the behaviour of each element was constant over time. For systems that don't meet these criteria, however, a holistic, or systemic, approach is more appropriate.

The client communication problem is a complex one, of course. Nevertheless, since history and culture have educated me to think in an analytical way, I often find myself taking an analytical approach to communication issues when a systemic one would be more appropriate.

Analytical versus systemic bug fixing

An analytical approach is appropriate when trying to fix a PC. I run a few diagnostics, identify the faulty board, and replace it.

However, I would not adopt such an approach when trying to solve a bandwidth issue across the internet. If the flow of information between two nodes were inadequate, I would look at the bandwidth of different major links and reason at a level way above that of the individual components of the internet. In other words, I would take a systemic approach.

When using a systemic approach, I begin from the assumption that the components of the organisation that I am dealing with are functioning normally. I don't really care what 'normal' is because, with a systemic hat on, my first concern is to find the information that will enable me to fix the problem in question, rather than understand its cause. I focus on future objectives, rather than the reasons for past failure.

I make no assumption that the action of any one person or thing underlies the problem. In any case, possible human causes of failure in the system are invisible to me (I cannot see inside people's heads). I am better off focusing on the things that can be seen and, perhaps, influenced—the relationships or links that hold the system together.

An analytical attitude to an email

I make an urgent email request to my parent organisation for information about a new product, but I get no answer. My first reaction may be that the person receiving the email has not understood it, or that they are overloaded, or they are lazy, or whatever. Then I might think perhaps the email did not arrive, or that it was badly worded. Maybe I will imagine that the product in question has problems—perhaps it can't be produced reliably, or there's a design flaw?

All of these possible responses have one thing in common: my worries are focusing on individual components of the system, searching for the point of failure. Further, my thinking is oriented towards the past and present states of the system, in an attempt to understand the cause of the delay. These are all characteristics of an analytical approach.

Characteristics and Advantages

Taking a systemic viewpoint helps in two ways. First, it relieves me of the difficult task of analysing what has happened. Second, it obliges me to take a step back and look for opportunities to 'tap the system with my hammer', to encourage it to produce what I need.

Taking a systemic approach cannot *guarantee* a successful resolution of all complex organisational problems, of course, but it is the appropriate strategy. It leads me to consider the problem at the right level of abstraction and spares me the frustration of trying to comprehend the incomprehensible. A brief summary of the characteristics of the systemic approach, contrasted with the analytical approach, is given in the table below.

Although the systemic approach is a vast subject, with much literature devoted to it, the reason for its popularity cannot be explained by any particular difficulty in the theory. Engineers are used to switching between different levels of abstraction in order to solve problems, modelling components in detail on some occasions and treating them as functional black boxes on others. We are used to working down from high-level specifications

Analytical approach	Systemic approach
Dualistic/binary/exclusive logic, characterised by 'or'—a thing is either right or wrong, black or white, good or bad.	Inclusive/continuous logic, characterised by 'and'—a thing has a degree of rightness and a degree of wrongness.
Linear causality—A affects B which affects C. Attempt to reduce the problem to isolated, time-invariant parts that can be treated independently.	Circular causality—A affects B and C, while B affects A and C, etc. Look at the system as a whole. Assume that its components change with time, and focus on the links between them.
To resolve a problem, the cause must first be found.	To resolve a problem, the objective must first be clarified.
Break down the objective into subobjectives in order to facilitate the resolution of the problem.	Look beyond the immediate objective ('objective N') to find the motivation for it ('objective N+1').
Search for errors and faulty components. Look for people responsible for the problem.	Search for resources that can help reach the objective (N or N+1). Look for people who can influence a solution.
Focus on the past to explain the present and hence find a solution for the future.	Project into the future to find a way of influencing in the present.

Getting things moving with a systemic approach

I am having difficulty getting a response from Harry in Product Engineering, and so I look for relationships in the 'system' that may help. Issues submitted to my company's online tracking system are always copied to Harry, and those that come directly from customers are marked 'urgent'. I therefore prompt my customer to make a request for information, coaching them on what to write. This is my 'tap with the hammer'.

The result will be, I hope, that Harry will either ask me to deal with the question, or will put me on copy when responding (since I am the CFE responsible for the account). Either way, I will have succeeded in unblocking my communication with him, and I should get an opportunity to talk to him about other needs (my original objective, which I have not defined for this example).

Note that a successful 'tap with the hammer' does not necessarily fix a problem. It perturbs the system in a way that favours my objective.

This approach contrasts with the traditional one of identifying the blockage in the system (Harry, perhaps?), and then attempting to fix it directly (e.g. more emails to Harry or escalation to Harry's boss).

(objectives) in some situations, using a process of gradual refinement, and to questioning high-level specifications in others (going from objective N to objective N+1 and beyond). When compared with standard engineering, software and mathematical practices, the systemic approach is hardly new.

In the domain of communication, however, the distinction of the systemic and analytical approaches and the advantages of the former when dealing with complex organisational problems do represent a breakthrough.[38] This is because our communication culture, inspired by the success of the scientific method, is strongly oriented towards analysis. A brief inspection of the table above may convince you of this. Doesn't it sound reasonable that, in order to solve a problem, one should look for its cause? That the faulty components and responsible people should be identified?

---

[38] This breakthrough is attributed to the Palo Alto school, a loose federation of psychologists working in the Bay area in the 1960s, and to Bateson in particular.

In some situations, this *is* the right approach, but in many others it is merely instinctive and inappropriate. This is why it is important to be conscious of the distinction between analytical and systemic strategies, and to be wary of my inclination for the former. If I find myself trying to dissect a complex situation, to discover what has gone wrong, who is responsible, etc., then I'm probably on the wrong track. In such circumstances, I need to take a step back, think systemic, and try to understand the system as a whole.

Systemic Approach using DISCOVER-Y and OAR

The DISCOVER-Y tool, presented in Chapter 5, defines eight zones, four of which describe the relationships between the elements of a system. By facilitating the representation of these links, thereby encouraging the user to consider them, the tool supports a systemic approach.[39]

By supplementing MAP with OAR in situations where my success depends on persuading colleagues to lend me a hand, I have essentially given MAP a systemic spin. In going from 'My objectives' to 'Our challenge', the focus has switched from the immediate objective to a higher one, and this is consistent with the systemic strategy of considering objectives associated with complex situations at the highest possible level.

Similarly, the focus on 'Resources' reflects the need to concentrate on possible contributors to a future solution, as opposed to looking for the causes of the current problem. In other words, it spends more energy on future solutions than on the history associated with current problems. Of course, the 'Plan' of MAP is also oriented towards the future, and having a plan certainly doesn't exclude a systemic approach. However, in this context, simply identifying possible inputs to a plan, in the form of resources, protects me from an excessive preoccupation with

---

[39] Tools that are dedicated to systemic analysis go one step further by defining a set of symbols to characterise the nature of the relationship between the two extremes of a link. For example, A is blocking B, A is supporting B, A and B have no communication.

detail. In a sense, I am asking the system[40] to provide me with a solution, nudging it with some well-chosen inputs, then stepping back to see what happens. I may then decide to nudge it again, and so on. This is the essence of a systemic approach.

Miscommunication with leadership (inspired by real events)

The diagram shows me, at the centre, working as a CFE team leader in the field, physically remote from my parent organisation, shown on the left, and supporting a local client, shown on the right. Things are not going well. Our competition is winning the client's business by demonstrating superior commitment—more CFEs available locally, greater responsiveness to the client's requests, greater attention at the senior executive level, a technology roadmap that is more closely in line with the client's needs than ours.

my_org   client_org

Believing that we are on the point of losing our foothold in the account (a foothold that had been hard to win), I decide to tackle my organisation and wake them up to the need to give us, the local CFE team, stronger backup. I write to the leadership team with a clear account of the opportunities and risks at the client account, and what the organisation needs to do in order to win the business from our competitors. My approach is direct, since my *analysis* of the situation is that the leadership team had not understood the difficulties of the field team. Consciously or subconsciously, I hold them responsible for the difficulties that we are facing.

The result is that the leadership team decide to discontinue its efforts to win the client account in question and, consequently, to close our local CFE office. There are no recriminations. My message was well received. It was clear enough, and had allowed the leadership to take an informed decision. But—and it is an enormous 'but'—that decision is exactly the opposite of what I had been hoping for.

---

[40] In the example above, the system is my parent organisation, including Harry and his Product Engineers.

Achieving a better outcome through a systemic approach

To show how a systemic approach differs from an analytical one, I will rework the miscommunication example from the text box on page 194. In this example, I am a CFE team leader in the field, physically remote from my parent organisation, supporting a local client.

Taking a systemic approach, I sketch the interactions between the parts of the situation, as shown in the diagram below. It reminds me that my parent organisation's main concerns are centred on a handful of big accounts.

In fact, three accounts bring in 80 per cent of the company's revenue. The other major influence on company decisions is the investors. A small, powerful minority own the bulk of the company stock. They actively control the board (and hence the leadership team) and strongly influence where funding is used.

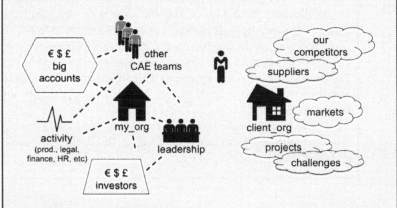

The current revenue from my local account is insignificant compared to that from the big accounts, and it will not move into the latter category anytime soon. Hence, understanding the leadership's priorities, I conclude that a direct appeal is unlikely to get results.

It then occurs to me that the CFE teams who deal with the big accounts work against more or less the same competition as us. It is also likely that the requests for support made by their accounts (e.g. for product improvements) overlap with ones that I receive—the big accounts are competing with my client in several markets, after all. My objective up to now has been to respond positively to as many of my client's requests as possible. What if I were to look beyond this?

Continued on next page ...

cntd.

My N+1 objective is to impress my client and displace my competition in the account. It might be possible to do this by exploiting work being done for the big accounts—to get an early warning of such work and to look for opportunities to use this locally.

I therefore make a couple of calls to CFE colleagues working on the big accounts, to see if they can help me. I find out about several product enhancements in the pipeline that I hadn't previously been aware of. They don't exactly match my client's requests, but they are close enough for me to credibly ask them for a discussion. Having agreed this with my client, I then write to the leadership team, but not with the apocalyptic message that I described for the analytical approach. Instead, I describe the situation, my concerns and the initiatives that I have taken. I don't press them for more resources, but I do explain the priorities I have chosen, given current resources.

Following these moves, the situation with my client does not change for some time. However, our foothold in the account remains firm, and we stay in touch with the client and their needs. I increase my visibility in, and visibility of, my parent organisation. Then one day my client is let down by one of their suppliers—my competition— and they ask me to help them out. This is the opportunity that I've been waiting for ...

Note that the main difference in the two versions of this scenario is not so much in the actions that I take as in my attitude: my actions are simply a consequence of that.

In Brief

✦ An important CFE dilemma is that, at the moment of making a commitment to an external client, it is not always possible to know how much backup will be available from one's parent organisation. There are:

- Challenges caused by a CFE's lack of control over resources

- Frustrations all round due to the difficulty that each collaborator has in envisaging the situation of the other.

✦ The OAR tool is useful when preparing to solicit help and collaboration from colleagues. It is used in conjunction with MAP and supports a systemic approach.

- 'Our challenge' focuses on a high-level objective, likely to be shared by my colleague.

- 'Audience', is the final beneficiary of the work being requested.

- 'Resources' are people and things that may influence the desired outcome.

✦ For complex problems, a systemic approach is often more appropriate than an analytical one:

- It focuses on objectives and factors that may influence the desired outcome, rather than on the causes of a problem and how to fix them

- It involves looking at a system as a whole—corrective action targets the links or relationships between the components of the system, rather than the components themselves.

11. Conclusion

'Everything should be made as simple as possible, but no simpler',
simplification of a statement by Einstein[41]

The ICON9® toolkit addresses the needs of engineers working in challenging commercial environments. By providing a structure for client encounters, it makes successful outcomes more probable, and it supports the continuous improvement of skills and processes. By providing tools for the job, it helps engineers to support clients efficiently while protecting their own interests and those of their organisations. By keeping the tools simple, it makes these benefits accessible to busy individuals and it allows them to be shared across teams.

An Open System to Build On

The ambition of ICON9® is to cover the essential aspects of communications for Customer-Facing Engineers with just a few tools, allowing others to quickly capture additional concepts by building on its structure and terminology. This is where the ninth icon comes in: it represents an open doorway into the system.

The number zero was not defined for use in mathematics until about the ninth century AD. Until then, calculations that we would consider trivial today were extremely difficult. This morsel of history shows the value of an adequate system for representing concepts that we wish to manipulate. The language that we use and the way that we organise ideas change the way we think, which changes the way we act.

---

[41] What Einstein actually wrote was (Einstein, CalapriceDyson 2011), 'It can scarcely be denied that the supreme goal of all theory is to make the irreducible basic elements as simple and as few as possible without having to surrender the adequate representation of a single datum of experience', which, it has to be said, is anything but simple!

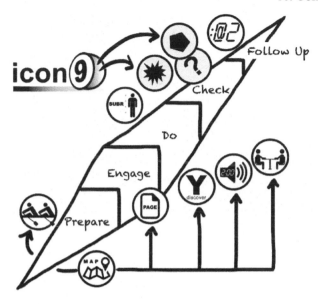

Just as important as the conceptual model are the methods that accompany it, and the skill to use them. A symbol to represent zero (the conceptual model) is of little value if it cannot be used to add, subtract, multiply and divide.

In the case of ICON9, the conceptual model is a representation of client encounters, composed of diagrams, vocabulary, tables and processes, with the corresponding set of methods, described in this book. Just as for mathematics, once the conceptual model and associated methods are understood, a great deal can be built on them.

For example, a CFE or an organisation that wishes to capture their method for product evaluations might exploit this opening. They could start from the Encounter Process, which suits the description of product evaluations very well, and add other features. To describe an evaluation, one would want to list the documents, hardware, software, etc. that are required at each step of the process (the inputs). Likewise, the items that are produced from each step must be defined (the outputs), as must the progress markers (the milestones) and the activities for each step. The result

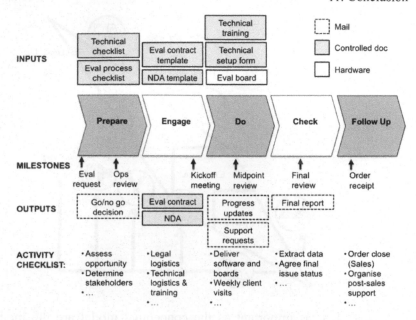

might be something along the lines of the diagram above.[42] Other ICON9 tools and concepts may be used within the listed activities, and to support the production of the input and output items required by the Evaluation Process. For example, DISCOVER-Y can be used in the Prepare step, to support the assessment of the opportunity and the identification of client-side stakeholders. The TMM will be used when producing many of the documents and presentations and, of course, MAP will turn up in many places.

When I work with companies to deploy the ICON9 system to their CFE communities, I find that each group has some specific requirements. For example, the ICON9 open door has been used to define tools and guidelines for:

▸ Technical trainers: defining training content, managing the training process and delivering courses

▸ Crossing cultures: adapting CFE communication styles to different national, generational and organisational cultures

---

[42] NDA = Non-Disclosure Agreement, a legal document that constrains parties receiving confidential information in its use.

▶ Time management: prioritising and scheduling multiple tasks while working under pressure, with deadlines to meet.

In addition to providing a foundation for new tools and guidelines, ICON9 has also been used for field projects that address a specific challenge. An example is given in the text box below.

Above all, the ninth icon of ICON9 symbolises flexibility. Each CFE has individual needs and opinions. While this book endeavours to take a 'generic' CFE perspective, it is still the result of a particular mix of work experience, education and DNA. I therefore encourage you to take advantage of ICON9's flexibility, adapt it to your style, to your team's needs and to the culture of your organisation.

ICON9-based sales kits (a real case)
I recently worked with a technology company to define a process for deploying product innovations to the field. The basic methods used by the Applications, Sales and Marketing teams were defined by ICON9 then, in addition, we developed sales kits for specific market segments. This included the creation of a generic kit—essentially an additional tool—from which new kits could be derived. The structure and use model of the kits leveraged ICON9's Discovery tools, as well as MAP and the TMM. The rapid creation and deployment of the kits was due to the starting point that ICON9 provided—the project did not waste time reinventing basics, and solutions were built upon the concepts that the reader has now seen.

Practice and Integration

Although each individual tool is simple in structure, there is a lot to learn in order to get the most out of the Toolkit. The following recommendations may help (Rackham 1988):

▶ Practise only one tool or method at a time.

▶ Try each new thing at least three times.

▶ Practise in (relatively) safe situations.

I would like to stress this last point. In a train-the-trainer course that I gave a couple of years ago to a UK-based company, I encouraged participants to punctuate long technical explanations with activities that would help their trainees to learn and have fun at the same time. One of my trainees happened to be giving training courses to their customers in China the following week. Inspired by our train-the-trainer course, they decided to change the normal presentation sequence, defined by their company, and try out some more entertaining, interactive activities. Thankfully, disaster did not ensue, but there were a number of difficulties. Ever since then I take care to emphasise the need to practise in safe situations!

The aim of practice is to go beyond simple intellectual understanding of a technique and achieve *integration*. This allows you to use the technique in multiple contexts and to adapt it without losing sight of its intent.

For example, once you have integrated the PAGE tool, then you will no longer depend on the acronym itself—you will know each of its four parts in the same way that you know where the accelerator, brake and clutch are in your car.[43] You don't think 'ABC—Accelerator Brake Clutch' every time you need to use the brake!

Thorough integration of a tool or method also allows you to exploit just a part of it, at an opportune moment. For example, if a colleague jumps to a discussion of actions too early in a conversation, then you can question them about the requirements (Needs) that these actions are supposed to meet. By doing this you are not using the SUBROUTINE process as such. However, by moving the discussion focus from actions to requirements you are applying the principles that underpin the tool.

Finally, a high level of integration of a tool or method is needed if you wish to promote its use by others, or even to explain your own use, as you are likely to receive both questions and resistance. You must therefore have some experience under your belt, and a robust understanding of the associated theory.

Good luck with all of this. I hope that your work on professional effectiveness is as rewarding as mine has been.

---

[43] Owners of automatic cars need not panic. This example works equally well without a clutch.

To Go Further

An online version of the Toolkit is available at:

http://www.icon9.net

These web pages include topics that space did not allow me to deal with here, as well as commentaries on past work in fields relevant to this text. In particular, there is an extended bibliography with a summary of each reference and appropriate links. Of course, references in the text may also be followed up using web-based search engines.

ANNEX

A1. DISCOVER-Y Exercise Solution

Part 1 (two to three minutes)

You are an engineer working for a small medical imaging company with responsibilities for technical support and technical marketing. A potential client tells you that they need an ultrasound scanner for use on the International Space Station (ISS). List the questions that you could ask them at an initial meeting.

Possible questions are listed below, organised by zone and by items in the zones. Please bear in mind that the idea of DISCOVER-Y is *not* to ask all possible questions—a large number are listed here by way of example only. Rather, DISCOVER-Y helps me to cover the most important elements of a situation during a conversation.

Part 2 (two to three minutes)

Draw the DISCOVER-Y diagram, number the zones, and complete zones 5 ('who') and 7 ('what') with the names of people, organisations, projects, products, as appropriate (zones 1 and 3 always represent the people in the meeting, called 'me' and 'the client' for simplicity).

In zone 5:
- Funding bodies
- Relevant groups in the client's organisation
- The client's competition for this contract
- The client's other suppliers (esp. competition for us).

In zone 7:
- The requested scanner
- The client's ISS project
- Concurrent, related projects
- Past, related projects.

Part 3 (two to three minutes)

Position the questions that you wrote in Part 1 in the appropriate zones, next to the name of the people, organisations, projects, etc. that they correspond to (e.g. by giving each question a letter and writing the letters in the zones).

For brevity, I have restricted the number of suggestions to three or four per zone and per item in zones 3 and 4.

Zone 1

As discussed in the text, I do not ask my client questions about this zone. Rather, I prepare answers for questions that I anticipate they will ask me. In doing this, I can imagine two branches of the DISCOVER-Y diagram that go off to the left, mirroring zone 5: 'who' and zone 7: 'what'. These are not usually drawn, since the DISCOVER-Y tool is oriented towards the client's situation, but it is worth remembering that, logically speaking, they are there.

With the above in mind, preparation related to zone 1 is rather like writing a Frequently Asked Questions (FAQ) text. In this case, we may anticipate questions about:
- Our corporate history and success stories
- Our scanner technology
- Our team.

Subjects to find out about

Zone 2
- Why the client approached my company
- What expectations the client has of my company (in the pre-sales, project implementation and deployment phases)
- What the client knows about my company and its techno.

Zone 3
- Client's responsibilities: position in their company and the project
- Client's past experience with this type of project
- Client's knowledge of scanner technology.

Zone 4
- The nature of the client company's relationship with the funding body(s)
- Any 'special relationships' with suppliers?
- Which internal groups actively influence the project in question (commercial and technical decisions)
- Is the client benchmarking suppliers?
- The client's criteria for supplier selection.

Zone 5

- Funding bodies
  - Have they committed to the project yet?
  - Any restrictions on sourcing (country of origin for parts and labour)
  - Reporting constraints.
- Relevant groups in the client's organisation
  - The company organisation in general
  - People in the project decision chain
  - Internal technical services, such as IT and Quality Control, that may affect the project.
- The client's competition for this contract
  - Competitor strengths and weaknesses
  - Client company's differentiators
  - Total Available Market and the client's part of it.
- The client's other suppliers (esp. competition for us)
  - Who they are
  - History of supply
  - Supplier's strengths and weaknesses.

Zone 6

- Funding body's level of interest in the requested scanner
- Other suppliers' attempts to bid for the requested scanner
- Other suppliers involved in the client's ISS project.

Zone 7

- The requested scanner
  - Is the machine to scan mice or men?
  - Which organs are concerned?
  - What kind of data output is needed?
  - What kind of screen?
  - What is the power budget?
  - What will be the acceleration at take-off?
  - Timeline.
- The client's ISS project
  - Scope of the project
  - Significance of the scanner to the project
  - Monetary value of the project
  - Timeline.

- Concurrent, related projects
  - Nature of the project
  - Any links to the ISS project
  - Timeline.
- Past, related projects
  - Nature of the project
  - Any links to the ISS project
  - Timeline.

Zone 8

- Client's level of personal commitment to the ISS project
- Client's implication in concurrent and past projects
- Client's personal preferences for discretionary items.

A2. Bibliography

Allen, David, 2001, *Getting things done*. New York: Viking.

Altucher, James, 2013, *5 Ways to Do Nothing and be More Productive*. 99u [online]. 2013. [Accessed 12 July 2015]. Available from: http://99u.com/articles/20576/5-ways-to-do-nothing-and-become-more-productive

Barnes, and Patterson, 2015, *A Necessary Evil: Edward Tufte and Making the Best of PowerPoint*. Thejuryexpert.com [online]. 2015. [Accessed 3 July 2015]. Available from: http://www.thejuryexpert.com/2011/11/a-necessary-evil-edward-tufte-and-making-the-best-of-powerpoint/

Baude, Dawn-Michelle, 2006, *The Executive Guide to E-mail Correspondence*. Career Press.

Berne, Eric, 1963, *The Structure and Dynamics of Organizations and Groups*. Grove Press.

Berne, Eric, 1964, *Games people play*. New York: Grove Press.

Berne, Eric, 1972, *What do you say after you say hello?*. New York: Grove Press, Inc.

Block, Peter, 2000, *Flawless consulting*. San Francisco: Jossey-Bass/Pfeiffer.

Care, John and Bohlig, Aron, 2002, *Mastering technical sales*. Boston, MA: Artech House.

Chapman, Alan, 2015, Businessballs free online learning for careers, work, management, business training and education. *Businessballs.com* [online]. 2015. [Accessed 3 July 2015]. Available from: http://www.businessballs.com

Cohan, Peter E, 2005, *Great demo!*. New York: IUniverse, Inc.

Cooper, Lynne and Castellino, Mariette, 2012, *The Five-Minute Coach*. New York: Crown House Publishing.

Cyborlink.com, 2015, International Business Etiquette and Manners for Global Travelers - Understanding cultural diversity, cross cultural communication, and intercultural business relationships for success. [online]. 2015. [Accessed 3 July 2015]. Available from: http://www.cyborlink.com

D'Ansembourg, Thomas, 2007, *Being genuine*. Encinitas, CA: PuddleDancer Press.

Delivré, François, 1997, *Question de temps*. Paris: InterEditions.

Delivré, François, 2004, *Le métier de coach*. Paris: Ed. d'Organisation.

Delivré, François, 2013, *Le Pouvoir de Negocier*. 3. InterEditions.

Dixon, Matthew and Adamson, Brent, 2011, *The Challenger Sale*. New York: Portfolio/Penguin.

Einstein, Albert, Calaprice, Alice and Dyson, Freeman, 2011, *The Ultimate Quotable Einstein*. Princeton: Princeton University Press.

Fisher, Roger, Ury, William and Patton, Bruce, 1991, *Getting to yes*. New York, N.Y.: Penguin Books.

Franklin, Benjamin, 2008, *The autobiography of Benjamin Franklin, 1706-1757*. Bedford, Mass.: Applewood Book.

Freeman, William, 2000, *A straightforward guide to the Two Minute Message*. London: Straightforward.

Guillaud, Hubert, 2011, *Comment prenons-nous nos décisions ?*. Le Monde [online]. 2011. [Accessed 4 July 2015]. Available from: http://www.lemonde.fr/week-end/article/2011/05/13/comment-prenons-nous-nos-decisions_1521812_1477893.html

Joule, Robert-Vincent and Beauvois, Jean-Léon, 2002, *Petit traité de manipulation à l'usage des honnêtes gens*. Grenoble: Presses universitaires de Grenoble.

Kahneman, Daniel, 2013, *Thinking, fast and slow*. Farrar, Straus & Giroux.

King, Stephen, 2000, *On writing*. New York: Scribner.

Kourilsky-Belliard, Françoise, 2008, *Du désir au plaisir de changer*. Paris: Dunod.

Lenhardt, Vincent, 2004, *Coaching for meaning*. Basingstoke, Hampshire: Palgrave Macmillan.

Rackham, Neil, 1988, *SPIN selling*. New York: McGraw-Hill.

Rock, David, 2009, *Your brain at work*. HarperCollins.

Rosenberg, Marshall B, 2003, *Nonviolent communication*. Encinitas, CA: PuddleDancer Press.

Saint-Exupéry, Antoine de, 1939, *Terre des hommes*. Paris: Gallimard.

Saint-Exupéry, Antoine de, 1948, *Citadelle*. [Paris]: Gallimard.

Schutz, William, 1994, *The Human Element*. Jossey-Bass.

Sobel, Andrew and Panas, Jerold, 2012, *Power questions*. Hoboken, N.J.: Wiley.

Steinbeck, John, 1975, *Steinbeck: a Life in Letters*. New York: Viking Press.

Stewart, Ian and Joines, Vann, 1987, *TA today*. Nottingham: Lifespace Pub.

Strunk, William, White, E. B and Kalman, Maira, 2005, *The elements of style*. New York: Penguin Press.

The Radicati Group, 2014, *The Email Statistics Report, 2014-2018* [online]. [Accessed 4 July 2015]. Available from: http://www.radicati.com/wp/wp-content/uploads/2014/01/Email-Statistics-Report-2014-2018-Executive-Summary.pdf

Tuckman, B. W. and Jensen, M. A. C., 1977, Stages of Small-Group Development Revisited. *Group & Organization Management*. 1977. Vol.2, no.4, p.419-427. DOI10.1177/105960117700200404. SAGE Publications

Tufte, Edward, 2003, PowerPoint is evil. *Wired* [online]. 2003. [Accessed 3 July 2015]. Available from: http://archive.wired.com/wired/archive/11.09/ppt2.html

A3. Detailed Table of Contents

215

217

Lightning Source UK Ltd.
Milton Keynes UK
UKOW04f1626080716

277943UK00011B/127/P